PRAISE FOR

"Each time I read a piece written by Ed Kemmick, I feel a compulsion to clip and save it or send it to someone else who would appreciate it as much as I do. And occasionally I am tempted to shoot it off to an individual who does not share Ed's and my opinions on things. You know, just to set them straight.

"Ed Kemmick's writings are informative, entertaining and insightful. I am so pleased that some of his excellent work has been incorporated in this book. I can now put the scissors away and just recommend to his admirers, and critics, 'Just read this.'

"I also understand that on occasion Ed plays a guitar. But hey, no one's perfect." — **Wallace McRae, Montana rancher and cowboy poet, author of** *Stick Horses and Other Stories of Ranch Life*

"Ed Kemmick has an uncanny knack for finding interesting people and bringing them to life with words. Kemmick writes with a wonderful blend of humor and insight, exploring the idio-syncrasies of human nature with his own unique worldview." — **Russell Rowland, author of** *In Open Spaces* **and fiction editor,** *New West Magazine*

"Ed Kemmick *is* Billings. Though I left Montana more than a decade ago, I read Kemmick online to stay connected to my hometown. For me, Kemmick's writing is as essential as the Rimrocks — and as ageless." — **Robert K. Elder, author of** *Last Words of the Executed* **and** *The Film That Changed My Life*

"Ed Kemmick is our David Brooks, our Keillor, even our Twain — solid on human nature, a keen analytical mind with just the right touch of whimsy." — **Marvin Granger, retired general manager (1984-2007), Yellowstone Public Radio**

"I'd make the argument that Ed Kemmick is Montana's pre-eminent journalist. He's a bulldog of a reporter, a superlative columnist and a damn fine writer. I look forward to a collection of his work. It's long overdue." — **Nick Ehli, editor-in-chief, _Montana Quarterly_**

"Ed Kemmick's a terrific newsman and observer of life, and it is impossible for him to write a dull column even when he tackles it without coffee at three on a Monday morning." — **Richard S. Wheeler, six-time Spur Award-winning novelist**

"Whether he's addressing an important subject in a serious manner or poking fun at the foibles of the human race, Ed Kemmick can always be counted on to inform, entertain, and delight his readers." — **Sue Hart, PEN Award winner for syndicated fiction and 2007 WILLA Award winner for creative nonfiction**

"Ed Kemmick is a Montana treasure. Each week, thousands look forward to his _City Lights_ columns like the first beer on Friday night. They settle the dust and remind us of what's truly important: love, laughter and the power of common sense." — **Dennis Swibold, University of Montana journalism professor and author of _Copper Chorus: Mining, Politics and the Press, 1889-1959_**

THE BIG SKY, BY AND BY

*True Tales, Real People
and Strange Times in the Heart of Montana*

Ed Kemmick

MISSOURI BREAKS PRESS

ISBN-10: 0982782233
ISBN-13: 9780982782231

The publisher and author are grateful to The Montana Standard, The Billings Gazette, Montana Quarterly and Parade magazine for permission to reproduce articles that originally appeared in those publications.

Printed in the United States

For Lisa, Jessie
Hayley and Pari

CONTENTS

CONTENTS

INTRODUCTION

I used to envy my brother because he was a carpenter. We'd be driving around town and he could point to his accomplishments — that house over there, a garage, that apartment complex. Others, too, could do this sort of thing. I think of the orthopedic surgeon who repaired my bum knee, and whom I often run into. He can look at me with some satisfaction, as at a job well done. Or imagine an emergency room doctor. He might see someone on the street and think, "I saved his life." A lawyer might see another person and think, "I kept that man out of jail."

The point is, what did I have? A few words on paper, destined for the dump or the recycling center. That's one reason I have always kept an old-fashioned clip file of everything I write, each story and column cut out and pasted into a spiral notebook. My colleagues look at me in disbelief — scissors and a glue pot in the 21st century? — but I persist, carefully snipping and preserving all my work. I now have something like 25 or 30 notebooks full of stories. They are my hedge against the transitory nature of journalism. They are my houses and garages, evidence, even if only for myself, that I have accomplished something in my life. And now a few of those pieces are making the leap from those clip files into this book.

The idea of putting together a collection of stories was suggested to me by Dick Dillof, a Paradise Valley resident better known as "Dobro Dick." I wrote about him in the spring of 2010, and in the course of several extended conversations with him, he told me he figured I'd written enough yarns about Montana characters to fill a book. After I'd thought about it awhile, I decided maybe he was right. I've been writing about such characters since 1980, when I went to work in the Anaconda bureau of The Montana Standard, published in Butte. I think back to one afternoon in the summer of 1981, when a call came into the Anaconda office. The caller was Vince Staiminger, a 90-year-old man who invited me out to his house. "Come on up and I'll tell you some stories," he said. A few days later I went, and for the next three hours Vince told me stories, stories that have now made their way into this book. All these years later, it still amazes me that I have managed to make a living out of listening to people tell stories and then, in their words and my own, presenting them to a larger world.

That's not all I've done, of course. I've also sat through hundreds, maybe thousands, of hours of meetings — city councils, school boards, county commissions, planning boards and half a dozen other august bodies. I've reported on budgets, covered speeches, sat through interminable public hearings and spoken with numberless cops, firefighters, dispatchers and EMTs. I've probably used the word "infrastructure" more times than is altogether forgivable. But through the years, I have always found the time to listen to stories.

Most of this book consists of profiles of people like Vince and Dobro Dick, but there are stories about Montana places, too, about Montana books and Montana history. I guess that means this book is about Montana. Maybe that's presumptuous of me, in a state where so many people can trace their roots back to the first generation of European settlers, or to the original inhabitants of this land. Me, I'm from Minnesota. I came out here in 1973, and except for a five-year stint back in the Twin Cities, I've been here ever since. I have lived in Bozeman, Missoula, Anaconda, Butte and now Billings. I've seen considerable stretches of Eastern Montana as part of my reporting job with The Billings Gazette, and once I spent a week driving from Yaak to Alzada, staying off pavement as much as possible. None of that makes me an expert on Montana. I am and will always be a transplant or "boomer," which is what the people of Anaconda used to call anybody who didn't inhale a whiff of smelter smoke with his first breath. But that's what newspaper reporters do. We might not know much ourselves, so we talk to people who do. In these pages, as you'll see, I've talked to a lot of Montanans, and to people who know a lot about this state. I have not included footnotes on any of the subjects covered in the book. It is safe to assume that some of the people I write about, like Vince Staiminger, who was 90 years old when I wrote about him in 1981, are no longer with us, but with some of the others I just don't know what happened to them. In a few cases, I have written individual introductions, telling the stories of how some of the stories came to be.

Take the story about Dobro Dick, for instance. It took me more than a decade from the first time I called him until we actually sat down for an interview. Another Gazette reporter, Mary Pickett, had spoken with Dick in the late 1990s, having heard about his amazing collection of antique musical instruments. Despairing of ever pinning him down to an interview, Mary turned her notes over to me, thinking maybe I'd have better luck.

For many years, it didn't look as though I would. I'd reach Dick by phone once or twice a year and he was always willing to talk, but mostly about other people he thought I should write about, including Lyle "Wild Horse" Cunningham, a cowboy singer and part-owner of a Miles City brothel; Halleck "Fiddler" Brenden, something of a musical prodigy and all-around eccentric genius; and "Railroad Dick" Garvey, a semi-retired hobo who had lived in Whitefish for many years and had opened his home to fellow tramps, itinerant folk musicians and other wandering souls.

In fact, Railroad Dick happened to be living on Dobro Dick's property, in an old caboose parked out behind his house, and did I want to talk to him? When I said yes, Dick put the phone down on a counter ... and then I waited and waited, for 20 or 25 minutes, until finally I heard, "Hello? This is Railroad Dick."

We had a fine conversation. I had ridden a few freight trains myself, which helped. I was never more than an occasional tramp-tourist, but I had been on a couple of extended freight-train trips and in fact I first entered the state of Montana in a boxcar. Railroad Dick agreed to be the subject of a profile, and we went so far as to make arrangements to ride a freight train together from Livingston to Laurel, accompanied by a photographer. I forget how my editor consented to this, but he did.

Well, it wasn't to be. I kept trying to get back in touch with Railroad Dick to work out the particulars, but all I got for the next year or two was Dobro Dick's answering machine. By the time I actually spoke with Dobro Dick again, Railroad Dick was long gone, I forget where. So I started working on Dobro Dick again, trying to arrange an interview. By then I had already written about Wild Horse Cunningham (see Page 133), and I would soon write about the death of Halleck Brenden (see Page 129). I think that's what pushed Dick over the edge. I'd done the stories he suggested, and many more of a similar nature, so he must have figured it was his turn.

I finally drove down to his place in the Paradise Valley in the spring of 2010, 12 years after our first phone conversation. I went there on a Friday morning and spent the next 27 hours in Dick's company, interrupted by five hours of sleep. I listened to dozens of good stories, watched Dick play 15 or 20 instruments and was shown all manner of weird curiosities, including a shrunken head. Sometime in the evening we drove off to the home of a Dutchman living farther down the valley. It was the fellow's 60th birthday, I think, and there was a lot of good food, good drink, and strangely interesting people. Dick played his Dobro and I played one of his very old Gibson guitars, the kind of guitar most people wouldn't allow out of the house, much less turn over to a virtual stranger at a Dutchman's birthday party. When I drove back to Billings the next day I felt exhausted, overwhelmed, and somehow privileged.

Thirty years after Vince Staiminger called me up, here I was again, amazed to think that this is what I'm paid to do — to spend time in the company of people like Dobro Dick and the other characters you'll meet in these pages, and then to distill their lives and adventures into something new, into stories on a page.

And speaking of characters, I have to mention one more before I turn you loose. Gazette photographer David Grubbs wasn't with me on the trip to the Paradise Valley, but that was one of the few reporting adventures I've had that he wasn't part of. I've been all over Montana with him and way up to Fort McMurray, Alberta. We've eaten a god-awful amount of bad food together, got lost, got bored to tears, damn near froze, drunk a few beers, stayed in motels that should have been condemned years earlier and once woke up in a tiny pink tow-behind camper so filthy and infested with mouse turds that if we hadn't staggered in there in the pitch-dark we never would have consented to sleep there.

Grubbs has been with me on at least a dozen occasions when we were talking to some first-class character, only to be told, "But you know who you really ought to talk to …" — rather in the manner of Dobro Dick telling me about Wild Horse Cunningham and Railroad Dick. And so Grubbs and I would take down a name or a phone number and sock it away until we were ready for another outing. I suspect we have a few more adventures ahead of us.

Ed Kemmick
Billings, Montana

DOBRO DICK: WANDERING TROUBADOUR

LIVINGSTON — Dick Dillof is nestled in an old leather armchair in the living room of his house near Livingston. In his lap is an odd-looking antique mail order instrument called a ukelin, also known as a prairie fiddle. It is a combination of a ukulele and a violin, but it sounds more like some kind of high-plains sitar. It is a many-stringed contraption that is alternately strummed, plucked and bowed, and in Dillof's hands it emits an ethereal, weirdly beautiful sound. When he finishes a brief song, the look of concentration on his face eases into a smile as he sits back in the chair.

"Look at this thing!" he says, holding up the ukelin. "Can you believe that sound? And they're nearly extinct."

Similar exclamations of wonder and delight are heard as Dillof performs on a succession of other instruments in his collection, some as outlandish as the ukelin and some as familiar as the guitar and banjo. And he plays them all. This is not a museum, and he's no curator.

"People say, 'You can even get a sound out of them,' " Dillof says. "Incorrect. You can get a beautiful sound out of them."

Dillof is nearly as passionate about the other artifacts and curiosities on display in his home — century-old photographs and calendars, cowboy gear and old books, a shrunken head from South America, a walking cane with a built-in violin, stuffed finches in a gilded cage that chirp when you wind a crank.

What they all have in common is that they are doors to vanished worlds. Play an ancient instrument, look into the eyes of a man in a 19th-century portrait, listen to finches that haven't sung for real in a hundred years, and who knows where you may end up. Dillof's life has been an effort to connect with what he has called "the unrecapturable American past." For 40 years, he has been a working cowboy, a roving troubadour, a sailor, a tramp and a compulsive wanderer.

"It was my dream to live that way," he says. "I don't know where it came from. It started with music, but then it went on from there."

Even now, at 57, he's not nearly ready to settle down. Gesturing around at his house, he says, "I see it as more of a home base than a home. If I didn't, I'd feel confined."

He distilled fragments of that wandering lifestyle into "Hobo," a mass-market paperback published in 1981, and he is at work now on a couple of other book projects. He also loves to draw, creating sketches as detailed and evocative as his short stories — a drifter sitting by a fire, tramps looking wistfully at a passing town through an open boxcar door, rough-looking men crowded around a dimly lit bar.

"I became like a walking sponge, soaking up songs and stories. And I got involved; sometimes in trouble. I wasn't just taking things in," he says.

Al Cantrell, an old musician friend who met Dillof on the Hi-Line in the 1970s and who now lives in Nashville with his wife and collaborator, Emily Cantrell, called Dillof "without a doubt the most eccentric person I know in the music business."

"In our circle," Emily says, "everyone likes to talk about Dick, what he's done lately or what he did 20 years ago that was phenomenal."

It began with a familiar dream: that of the East Coast kid who wanted to head out West to the land of cowboys, open prairies and big skies. Dillof, who grew up in New York and spent time on a Vermont dairy farm, grew restless and headed west at 19, seeking adventure. He already played banjo by then, as well as the Dobro, similar to the Hawaiian guitar, which he played well enough to earn the nickname "Dobro Dick." He found work on a cow ranch in the Missouri Breaks, where he learned to ride and rope. It was also there that he heard, for the first time, old-time western music played by real cowboys. He worked the High Plains, on ranches in Montana, Wyoming and Idaho, with winters off so he could tour with western-swing bands doing the dance hall circuit.

Al Cantrell met Dillof in 1975, when Cantrell was playing in Shelby with a country-western band called Honey and the Hi-Liners. At 3 a.m., after a show, Dillof pulled up in the parking lot of the bar where they were playing. He was driving a VW square-back jammed full of all his worldly possessions, which included even then an astonishing variety of instruments. He was proficient on the Dobro, Cantrell recalls, but he was also "quite the showman on the autoharp and banjo." In fact, he said, Dillof's skill level and showmanship seemed better suited for "The Gong Show" than a working country band, but they couldn't resist, and Dillof soon joined the group.

There would be many other bands and much more touring. He has performed with Patsy Montana, Vassar Clements and Ramblin' Jack Elliott, and when he played at Bill Monroe's Brown County Jamboree in Indiana, the posters gave big billing to "Dobro Dick," no last name needed, "in person from Montana."

One of his bands, Dobro Dick and the Red Brothers, played for a crowd of several hundred thousand when they represented the American West at a Voice of Asia Music Festival in Kazakhstan.

After picking up the "rambling habit" as a musician, Dillof discovered freight trains, quickly becoming hooked on that mode of transportation. Drawing inspiration from the writings of Jack London and Woody Guthrie, he also began writing on the road, setting down his thoughts and stories "in bunkhouses, fleabag hotels and on the rails." That eventually grew into his "Hobo" collection, which led to a film, with his music, called "Lonesome Whistle Blow."

Though most people still know him as Dobro Dick, his nickname on the rails was "Rattlesnake Dick." He was no light traveler. He used to hit the rails packing several instruments, a sketch pad and a folding typewriter. Sometimes he traveled with a ventriloquist's dummy. The dummy, he said, did the fast talking to get him past big yard bulls.

He soon added another form of travel to the mix, recruiting some musician friends to rent a sailboat and go island-hopping in the West Indies or the Northwest for a month or so, paying for most of the trip by performing at bars and clubs along the way. It's something he still does every few years.

It's been a while since Dillof did any cowboying and more than a decade since he's ridden freight trains — contemporary security concerns make it difficult, he says — but he still travels with his teardrop trailer, towed behind a car. "Rubber-tramping," as he calls it, is more comfortable, and he can tote many of his instruments along. The custom-made teardrop trailer, handsome as it is, is not just for show.

"It sets your spirit up differently to travel that way," he said. "These rolling homes are not just novel; they're essential to my traveling. A Pullman sleeper with a ship's galley and an awning to play music under — they're the perfect minstrel-mobile."

In addition to "Lonesome Whistle Blow," Dillof had a small part in Robert Redford's "A River Runs Through It," which was filmed mostly in the Livingston area. He and the Cantrells formed the string band shown performing at a church picnic in the movie.

Through most of those wandering years, the Livingston area was the place Dillof came back to. For 10 years he parked an old sheep wagon in the Paradise Valley and lived there when he wasn't on the road. Eventually, he says, "I upgraded my domicile, my lifestyle, to a caboose." For a few years the caboose was parked on property next to the home of the late Richard Brautigan, a novelist who often lit up the Paradise Valley with his semi-legendary sprees and escapades.

Greg Keeler, a Montana State University English professor, author and songwriter, regularly played music with Dillof at Brautigan parties. Keeler also devoted a short chapter to Dillof in "Waltzing with the Captain," his book of reminiscences about Brautigan. He described Dillof as "a mysterious old-style musician, cowboy drifter" who played "every song and instrument from sea chanteys on the squeeze box, to ditties on some weird

Middle-Eastern sounding bow-played instrument."

In an interview, Keeler said the late poet Ed Dorn used to call Dillof "the ubiquitous Dobro Dick. He seemed to be everywhere and nowhere all at once. ... He seemed like he was out of another century."

About 10 years ago, Dillof moved into a house. There, between occasional gigs and assorted wanderings, he continues to delve more deeply into music of the past.

Among his instruments are variations of the autoharp, including one he describes as being "in the family of one-man-band zither-like contraptions." Many of the instruments came from old Sears and Montgomery Ward catalogs, and many of them ended up in lonely homesteads where there was a scarcity of musicians to play accompaniment. Dillof has a ukulele with a harp attached, old concertinas, harmonicas with sundry attachments, a folding banjo that's perfect for traveling, something called a guitarophone and something else called a dolceola, a kind of zither with a tiny keyboard appended to it.

In a 30-year search, Dillof found two dolceolas, both of them "trashed beyond recognition."

"I traded one to a luthier up in Michigan in exchange for having him restore the second one — a meticulous job which took three years," he says.

There's no one around to show Dillof how to tune half these instruments, much less how to play them, so he just figures it out. How?

"You become obsessed," he says. "You just do it. And when you get it, you got it."

One instrument cherished more for its history than its playability is a fiddle hand-carved with a jackknife by a Basque sheepherder from the Big Timber area. On its back are two paintings of the same woman — one fully clothed and the other half-naked. The old sheepherder's lonely longings are almost palpable.

Upstairs, in a guest room, Dillof asks, "Are you ready for trouble?" This is his way of introducing another prized possession, an old Edison cylinder player, which operated on the same principle as the later record player, except that the audio was recorded and played on a hollow wax cylinder rather than a flat disc. An engineer with Edison Laboratories in New Jersey still occasionally records contemporary musicians on wax cylinders, and some years ago he made a recording of Dillof playing a fast-paced swing tune on one of his Hawaiian guitars.

"I consider it an honor and a great privilege to be recorded on wax cylinder, an honor greater than any other recording I've done," he says.

He puts the needle on the spinning cylinder and out of the wooden amplification horn comes a cascade of music that might be 100 years old — tinny, high pitched and impossibly antique. Next to the Edison is an old brass lamp, whose central stem is a hula dancer in a grass skirt. Dillof pulls the chain and she starts dancing, swaying her hips to the music. Dillof has a faraway look on his face, something between awe and ecstasy.

"I always wanted to go back in time," he says. "I finally got to."

Originally published July 18, 2010, in The Billings Gazette

STONEVILLE SALOON:
LAST STOP IN THE MIDDLE OF NOWHERE

This story was the last installment in a seven-day "Yaak to Alzada" series that ran in The Gazette in October 1999, chronicling another of my adventures with photographer David Grubbs. We spent seven days driving from Yaak, in the far northwestern corner of Montana, to Alzada, the last town in the southeastern corner. We did so, as we said in the introduction to the series, because in Montana "Yaak to Alzada" is shorthand "for border to border, A to Z, a means of hinting at the immensity and diversity of a state that is also a state of mind."

We drew a diagonal line from Yaak to Alzada on a map of Montana, then stayed as close to that line as we could while driving as little as possible on paved roads. Beyond that, we deliberately made no plans. Assorted colleagues threw suggestions at us — story ideas, people to visit along the way, must-see features, etc. — but we resisted every temptation to set anything up. Our goal was simply to drive and see what we could find, to let the road be our guide. This seemed like a brilliant idea ... until we arrived in Yaak, a tiny hamlet that was home to little more than a laundry, a small grocery store and a bar, the Dirty Shame Saloon. The laundry and the store were all but dead, so we went into the Dirty Shame, which at mid-afternoon was also nearly empty. We had a look around, talked to the bartender, made small talk with the few customers and, for lack of anything better to do, had a beer. We'd been there for more than an hour, with the afternoon slipping away, and all at once our refusal to make any plans seemed insanely irresponsible. I was beginning to panic as I made my way out to the deck, which looked out over a blue-black ocean of timber. I was standing there in despair, not enjoying my beer at all, when a man walked up to the railing beside me. His name was Pirate, maybe 50 years old, bearded, grizzled, wearing a black P.O.W. T-shirt. He cocked his head, looking up at a blue sky streaked with white vapor trails.

"Know what those are?" he asked.

"Um, contrails?" I said.

"Nope," he answered. "Those aren't contrails. It's poison, sprayed by our government. It's all part of the New World Order. King Clinton."

Out of the corner of my eye I could see Grubbs approaching, so I spun around and gave him a thumbs-up, mouthing the word "Bingo!"

On the rest of our weeklong trip we had a few more difficult days scraping up something to write about, but there was nothing quite like the panic and subsequent exhilaration of standing on the deck of the Dirty Shame. I wanted to include at least one story from that series, mainly because our week on the road, followed by a week of intensive writing, was one of the prime experiences in my career. I decided to use the story from the last day of our adventure, which ended, as it had begun, in a bar with a wonderful name.

ALZADA — Driving southeast, Alzada is the last town on the way out of Montana.

But Alzada doesn't feel like the end of anything. It's more like the T-shirts say in Alzada's Stoneville Saloon: "Conveniently located in the middle of nowhere."

In Montana, even the middle of nowhere is beautiful. It might be prairie, but it's not the flatlands. There are rolling hills, rough pyramids of shale, and in the distance pillars of eroded rock and a matching set of flat-topped buttes. Thick stands of trees march along the banks of the nearby Little Missouri River, and from Alzada you can see the western end of the Black Hills.

In the Stoneville Saloon on this Saturday morning, a truck driver from Georgia named Tiny is having trouble just seeing the pile of change in his hand, the only cash he's got left after a Friday night in the saloon. But Tiny, who isn't, has no complaints. He'd fetched his guitar out of his truck about 11 p.m. Friday and banged on it till 2 a.m., having so much fun his fingers still hurt this morning.

He said he was trucking a load of gaming machines from Bozeman to Philadelphia and finally managed to roll through Alzada when the Stoneville Saloon was open. He'd been hearing about it for years, he said, and now he knew why truckers all over the country had been recommending it.

That's just what Rob Peterson and Diane Turko want to hear. They moved to Montana in 1991, bought the Old Stand tavern and transformed it into the Stoneville Saloon, named in honor of the handle Alzada wore back in Montana Territory days. It got its name back then from Lou Stone, who happened to own a saloon, but it was changed in 1885 to Alzada, in honor of Mrs. Alzada Sheldon, the wife of an area rancher.

The Stoneville Saloon sits at the junction of highways 212 and 323, on the edge of town. The town itself consists of a gas station-convenience store, a no-name cafe, a tire shop, a handful of houses and half a dozen abandoned buildings.

Rob and Diane moved here from Huntington Beach, Calif., after passing through on vacation and falling in love with the blue skies and big, open country. It's not very likely that even after eight years in Alzada anyone is going to mistake them for natives. On this Saturday, Diane is wearing a sleeveless black T-shirt and leopard-skin shorts, short enough to show off her many tattoos. Her tightly braided blond hair falls down to the middle of her backside and she's wearing heavy black boots.

Rob's also wearing a sleeveless T-shirt, a bandanna festooned with skulls and a golden beard that hangs down past his belt buckle. His arms are covered in tattoos.

"I'm pretty hard not to recognize," Diane says.

"We kind of stand out in a crowd," Rob adds.

Nevertheless, Rob says, most of the locals have come to accept them. The younger people started coming in first, he says, "but we've got some of the old folks, too. I mean the dyed-in-the-wool, hard-ass cowboys." That's as it should be, he says. He and Diane are doing what most everybody else in rural Montana does: trying to scratch out a living, trying to make enough money to continue living in Montana.

"It's pretty tough here," Rob says. "If you can make it here, you can probably make it anywhere."

When they moved to town, he says, the Old Stand was "one of those one-light, local, don't-come-in-here places." They worked hard to make it more attractive, adding a Western front and hitching posts, advertising far and wide, starting their own Web page and stuffing the saloon with antiques, novelties and posters. They sell hats and T-shirts, ammo, hunting and fishing licenses, ostrich burgers and a justly famous bowl of chili.

There's a bandstand for the occasional live show, and it doubles as Diane's tattoo parlor. She tattoos some truckers and bikers, she says, but mostly it's just folks from the area, cowboys and cowgirls from all over southeastern Montana and the corners of Wyoming and South Dakota.

Business is pretty steady all year, Rob says, but things get downright crazy around the time of the annual motorcycle rally in Sturgis, S.D., which is just 62 miles away. On the Wednesday before each rally, bikers stop at the Stoneville on their way to Sturgis from Hulett, Wyo., which throws a big pig roast for rally-goers.

On the Wednesday before the rally this August, Rob says, he had 5,000 motorcycles parked around the saloon at one point, and he sold 46 cases of beer in one hour.

On the land they bought with the saloon, Rob and Diane have a trailer they live in and enough acreage for Diane to raise some pigs and sheep. Diane says the first winter was a shock, but they've gotten used to it. She still hasn't entirely gotten used to the wind.

"It blows every day," she says. "Some days worse than others, but it blows every day."

Rob enjoys just standing behind the bar and holding forth — on any topic under the sun. Late last night and early on this Saturday, he's unburdened himself of opinions on everything from RUBs (rich urban bikers) and Fudds (or hunters, as in Elmer Fudd) to the lack of a proper Montana history curriculum in state schools.

But Rob doesn't just talk, he listens, and he says living in Alzada has been "a learning curve, for us and the locals." One thing he's learned is that a Californian can find contentment in the wide-open spaces of the interior West.

Or, as he says, "It's an area and a life that kinda grows on you."

Originally published October 9, 1999, in The Billings Gazette

HIKING WITH BOB:
LIES IN THE GREAT OUTDOORS

You don't need many supplies for a day hike up a mountain, but there are some essentials. Before setting out to climb Going-to-the-Sun Mountain in Glacier National Park, my brother-in-law and I made sure we had water, food, bug repellent, bear spray, rain gear and some spare clothes.

As important as all those items were, I'm sure I would never have contemplated the climb, nor completed it, without those most valuable supplies of all — lies.

If my brother-in-law didn't lie to me about the difficulty of the hike, and if I didn't lie to myself every 20 minutes or so as I labored up that steep face of broken shale, I never would have stood on the summit at last, looking out at the dozens of peaks that have been called the crown of the continent.

My brother-in-law, whose name is Bob Hughes and who lives in Missoula, doesn't need to lie to himself. He always knows what he's getting himself into, and if the escapade involves a strenuous climb or dangerous weather, or any kind of obstacle or peril you can think of, all the better as far as he's concerned.

Deep down I must feel stirrings of the same impulse, because I do allow myself to be talked into hiking with Bob. I just need to be lied to first. When Bob tells me we're going on a "short" hike, that the going won't be "too hard," that the mountain "isn't all that steep," I stand there like a yokel listening to a barker on the midway: "One buck! Three balls! How could you NOT break those plates!"

I know Bob's lying, just as surely as the yokel knows he's not going to break those plates, but the yokel hands his dollar over to the barker and I hand my carcass over to Bob.

On the drive to Glacier Park from where I was staying with my family on Flathead Lake, I had time to think of other hikes I'd been on with Bob. Four years earlier we had gone into the Rattlesnake Wilderness north of Missoula, and for once Bob might have been telling the truth when he said it would be an easy hike.

It would have been if we had stayed on the trail. But then Bob got it into his head to check out a lake we saw in the distance, which meant scrambling down a long, steep ravine full of loose rock and dense brush. To avoid going up the same way, we swung around to find a better route to the ridge, bushwhacking long and hard to reach the trail again.

Then we started hiking in the wrong direction just as it began to rain, which cost us another hour by the time we realized our mistake and backtracked. (I swear we lost an hour, but Bob says it was 15 minutes. It has become such a habit with him that he lies even in retrospect.) We trudged through a soaking rain for the last two hours of the hike, thoroughly drenched and slipping constantly on the muddy trail.

There were times when I would gladly have lain down to rot in the woods, but Bob sustained me with a steady stream of falsehoods: "It's just a little farther," "I think we'll be able to see the car after this next bend," "It could be a lot worse," etc., etc.

A year after that, he and a couple of friends invited me to climb a mountain just outside Missoula. This was to be, naturally, a very brief climb, a cake walk, a short "grunt" rather than an actual hike. Here again, Bob was not lying outright: if you hiked all the time and had iron legs, what he said would have been true.

And as I soon learned, "grunt" is actually a technical term, which describes a short, brutal climb straight up a small mountain, intended as a workout for imminent excursions of greater severity.

This supposed mountain was little more than a sheer, tree-less incline covered with tufts of grass and scree, perfect terrain for the bighorn sheep we saw but no place at all for a human be-ing. There wasn't a tree in sight until we finally got to the top — and the top had recently been clear-cut, reduced to an ugly jum-ble of stumps, slash piles and mounds of dirt.

None of this mattered to Bob and his friends. It was just a grunt, and it got them in shape. For my part, stumbling down the mountain was far worse than the climb up, and left my thighs so strained and sore that I could barely walk down stairs for the next couple of days.

Before this summer's outing, our most recent climb was to the top of another Glacier Park peak, Mount Siyeh, described by Bob in reassuring tones as "the easiest 10,000-foot peak in the park." This, if nothing else, was a real mountain, though it looked hardly more attractive than the one near Missoula. It rises up from the forest like a big brown sheet, featureless but for a few patches of snow, stretches of steep ground strewn with thin fragments of broken rock and ledges of stone that cut across the face of the mountain like the walls of a fortress.

Although I was half dead by the time we reached the top, our reward for four hours of misery was an unforgettable view. The front side of Siyeh may be nearly blank, but at its back it drops straight down 3,000 feet or more, and at the bottom is Cracker Lake, a pool of brilliant green pierced on one side by the knife-like edge of an advancing glacier.

Unfortunately, we had all of 15 minutes to enjoy the view. The threatening clouds that we had seen in the distance all day were suddenly speeding toward us, churning and spitting out rain. We stuffed our gear into our day packs just as a cloud, or the mist that clouds are made of, came boiling up from the back side of Siyeh, curling over the ridge at a pace faster than I could run.

A few minutes earlier Bob and I had been casually discussing the most likely way to descend, but now we simply charged down the mountain via the straightest route we could find.

The rain turned to a stinging sleet and then to wind-driven slush as we clambered down a narrow chute of crumbling shale. It would have been difficult even if it hadn't been soaking wet; as it was, the route was preposterously difficult. But since the only alternative seemed to be freezing to death on the side of the mountain, we pressed ahead.

Two hours later we were at the car. I was cold and wet, dog-tired and delirious, covered with scratches and bruises. It was only then that I remembered Bob had originally suggested bringing along my middle daughter, who was then 11. He must have known she'd never come, but the seed, the fiction, had been planted: How could I question a hike that Bob thought my 11-year-old daughter could handle?

With all that history to consider, it is fair to ask how I could swallow Bob's lies again as we made our way to Going-to-the-Sun Mountain. And yet I did. I had been looking forward to a hike for months, but I needed to be soothed with the salve of untruth before agreeing to join Bob on this year's adventure.

He did not let me down. Going-to-the-Sun Mountain, he assured me, was not nearly as high as Siyeh. Better yet, Bob went on, it was "only" 4,000 vertical feet from the trailhead to the peak, and he had read in a book somewhere, or maybe he heard it from a friend, that the ascent of Going-to-the-Sun was far less difficult than Siyeh, over much better ground, and would take "a couple of hours" at most.

Fortified by his torrent of fables, we started up the trail at 11 a.m. on a perfectly clear, hot August day, accompanied by Bob's friend from Polson, Bob Long. This second Bob was as much a billy goat as my brother-in-law, and I'm sure if I hadn't been there to slow them down, they would have raced each other up the mountain, stopping now and then to take a quick drink or to nibble on some lichen.

It was on this hike that I realized how often I lied to myself while accompanying Bob. There was no way I could stand at the bottom of Going-to-the-Sun Mountain and admit the naked truth: "There it is, 4,000 feet straight up through pulverized shale to a peak you can't even see from here."

I had to break the mountain into sections, and lie my way through each one. At the start, walking easily over the groomed trail, I told myself that maybe there was a good trail all the way to the ridge. But we were off the trail in half an hour, cutting across an overgrown meadow that took us to the base of the mountain.

Listening to the two Bobs plan our ascent, I let myself believe they were seeing an easy way up. Minutes later we were climbing a steep ravine, clutching shrubs and struggling for handholds in the rock, and I told myself that surely this was the last of this kind of climbing we'd see. When we reached scree I was relieved by a change in terrain, until my ankles began sliding this way and that, and once more I convinced myself that this particular hell would soon be over.

And so it went. I told myself I was always tired at first and would get a second wind. I told myself I wouldn't run out of water and could guzzle at will. I told myself that if I didn't get a second wind pretty damned soon I was just going to quit and meet the Bobs on the way down. I told myself five or six times that the point of rock I could see had to be the peak, and when we finally did reach the summit I told myself the crowning lie, that the descent, at least, would be easy.

I knew that the descent is always hardest on me, especially when it involves slipping and half-jogging on rubber legs down an unstable mountainside of shattered rock, but the big lie helped me enjoy half an hour of peace on the summit.

On the way down I didn't even try lying to myself. It seemed pointless by then. I was aching from top to bottom, lightheaded and parched — we had drunk the last of our water on the peak — so I let gravity pull me on, paying just enough attention to avoid a tumble.

We reached the car about 5 p.m., a mere six hours after starting up the mountain, and a few minutes later I was sitting barefoot on a low stone wall along Going-to-the-Sun Road, drinking a beer and staring up at the mountain we'd just come down.

Here was the moment that will stick in my mind when the aches and pains and next-to-dead weariness are a distant memory. Finally, when I had no further reason not to, I told myself the truth: It had all been worth it, every miserable step, and I couldn't wait to go again next year.

Originally published August 21, 1997, in The Billings Gazette

ADVENTURES IN BOOK-BUYING

The Mai Wah Building on Mercury Street in Uptown Butte is a Chinese cultural museum these days, but when I lived in Butte in the early 1980s, the main room on the ground floor housed a junk shop. The first time I saw it, the store was closed, so I pressed my face to the window to see what was inside. What I saw, amid the heaps of tools, battered home furnishings, tennis racquets, bottles and decomposing rugs, was a small collection of books.

To me, there is nothing more promising than a collection of old books, especially when seen like this, dimly, from a distance. At that moment there is always a chance, however infinitesimally small, that one of them is a first edition of "Moby Dick," inscribed by Melville, or, since we're in Butte, maybe a journal that belonged to Wobbly martyr Frank Little, murdered by gun thugs in 1917. Or – and why be restrained in that first wild moment of imagining – what if I stumble upon the lost book of Cicero, that single manuscript once owned by Petrarch, lent to a friend and never seen again?

You never know. Even after decades of disappointment I still allow myself to hope.

A sign in the window said that if the shop was closed, to

knock on the door at the top of the stairs, which were just to the left of the main entrance. As I began to make my way up, the first couple of stairs creaked under my weight. In response, from behind the door above, there erupted a furious racket of barking and snarling, as if somebody had touched a cattle prod to a dog already predisposed to unpleasantness. He attacked the door, too, throwing his body against it and tearing at it with his claws. I stood there frozen, wondering if I should proceed. The door didn't look particularly strong. What if the dog broke it down, or pushed it far enough to slip out? All indications were that I would be ripped to pieces before I could even turn around.

But those books. ... You just never knew. And so I kept climbing, clutching the railing to support my trembling legs. With each step the dog reached a new pitch of fury, but I made it to the landing at last and timidly knocked on the door, as if the junk shop owner, if he were home, hadn't been sufficiently alerted to my presence already. When he did finally come to the door, he didn't open it, but shouted out, "Who's there?"

"Nobody," I said. "I mean, nobody you know. I just wanted to look around your shop."

We were both screaming to be heard above the barking of the dog, and when the man wasn't speaking to me he was cursing at the dog.

"My shop?" he shouted. "What do you need?"

"Well," I said, feeling as if I had already let him down some-how, "I just wanted to look around."

There was silence for a moment, then another communication.

"I'm busy right now."

Busy? I said to myself. Busy? What, making a bomb? Butchering some unfortunate urchin?

"Come back tomorrow," he said. "Noon."

So, I went back the next day, repeating the whole terrifying scene. The dog seemed even more enraged than the day before. But I knocked again and told the owner, whom I still hadn't seen, that I was the fellow he had told to return today. He seemed doubtful, but eventually he opened the door a crack, a crack into which the snarling dog inserted his snout, slobbering, growling and barking. The man whacked the dog on the head and then pushed him away with his foot as he slowly squeezed himself through the slightly open door, all the while swearing and threatening. He got through at last and slammed the door shut, and the dog, as if this were a game with regular rules, immediately stopped barking.

The man before me was tall and very lean, hawk-faced, with black glasses taped at the extremities, intense blue-gray eyes, and a jaw so distinct and angular that it looked detached, like something from an archaeology dig.

"I'm sorry about Scout," he said. "He doesn't like people. Hell, he doesn't even like me. Now, what it is you were interested in?"

"Books," I said, looking up at him from a couple of steps below the landing. "I like books."

He eyed me sharply, as if he thought I was being funny, or was trying to pull something over on him.

"I don't have many books. But I suppose you can have a look. Come on."

I let him pass and he led the way downstairs. He opened the door to the junk shop with an old skeleton key, held it open and motioned me inside. As soon as I got within a few feet of the small shelf of books and had a better look, I figured it was hopeless. They all looked like books that had suffered some water damage and then been stored somewhere very cold, somewhere susceptible to mold. But I felt obliged to look at each title, and to pull a couple of volumes off the shelf for closer inspection. I was getting nervous because after putting the owner to so much trouble, it would have been awkward to leave without making a purchase. Then I saw a title I was actually interested in: "Among the Nudists" by Frances and Mason Merrill.

It was mildewy and warped and the orange cloth covers were in bad shape, but it looked too odd to pass up. It turned out to be an examination of the culture of Nudism, published in 1931 and illustrated with black-and-white photographs of naked men engaged in a tug-of-war, naked families playing with enormous medicine balls and circles of naked men and woman cavorting in a glen. Except for the nakedness of all present, the photos looked like something out a Soviet compendium of healthful proletarian pursuits. A few samples showed the prose to be very serious and sober-minded, deliberately avoiding the least hint of titillation or salaciousness. I was almost certain I'd never read it, but I also knew it would make a great conversation piece, especially since I had more or less risked my life to look at it.

"How much for this one?" I asked, and when he saw the title he looked at me funny again, trying to decide whether I was a wise guy, or whether, God forbid, I had something more unseemly in mind. I hoped he wasn't considering siccing his dog on me. But at last his instincts as a merchant overcame his doubts and he said, "Three bucks."

At that time, three bucks was too much for a book in that condition, and three bucks would have bought me two beers in the Silver Dollar Saloon next door, but I had to make a purchase and this book was the only one I wanted. So I paid up, we walked outside, he locked the door and then he went back up the stairs, back to his rabid companion.

It was one of the strangest transactions in what is now a 40-year hobby of buying used books, but it was also a good reminder of why I collect them. I spoke above about the possibility of finding something rare and valuable in the junk shop, but there's more to it than that. I just happen to love old books, the way they look and feel and smell. I don't scorn paperbacks, but generally speaking I want to have in my hands a book that is worthy of its contents. There have been certain great works of literature that I could not bring myself to read for many years, until I managed to find them in suitably attractive editions. They are easy enough to find these days — just a click or two away on eBay or Amazon. Too easy, I think. I still enjoy the hunt, the anticipation, the idea that any odd collection, whether in a junk shop, garage sale or thrift store, might hold a book that has been waiting for years, just for me.

Even not buying a book is sometimes an adventure. Not far from the Mai Wah in Uptown Butte was a secondhand store run by a fellow known as Tony the Trader. He had a huge collection of curios, treasures and oddball collectibles, including some good books. But nothing, as I recall, had a price tag on it. If you asked, Tony would rap his finger on his noggin and say, "I got all the prices right here." So I'd ask him, "How much for this book?", knowing the volume in question was worth maybe five bucks, and Tony would hold it up, squint at it, scratch his head and say, "That one's $37. It's a good book."

And so it went with every book, and I never bought a thing from him. Though I don't know for sure, I assume he was like that with everything in the store. I would find out in time that it's not unheard of in the secondhand business for merchants to be unwilling to part with their wares. Some of them are collectors who open stores to convince themselves they are not hoarders, or perhaps to convince their spouses of the same. Whatever the case, Tony's books were in no danger of leaving the store. I will say this for Tony, though: At least he let me look.

There used to be a bookstore in downtown St. Paul, Minn., in which not even looking was allowed. The store in question was a jumble of dangerous-looking stacks of books, books that looked as though they hadn't even been sorted, just tossed in at random from the front door. What made this establishment unique, as far as I know, was that the proprietor apparently wasn't willing to let people in. I suppose there could have been something about me personally, but all I know is that I went there on at least three occasions and never got past the front door. The owner (I guess it was the owner) was a very large man, dressed in denim overalls and a white T-shirt, who sat in a folding chair right in the entryway, between two large windows, so there was no way around him unless he moved. He'd sit there smoking cigarettes and reading the paper, and if you walked up and stood in front of him, he'd wait a few long moments before looking up, and even then he didn't seem to be acknowledging your presence so much as wondering what was casting a shadow on his newspaper.

The first time I went there, silly me, I thought I'd browse. Nothing doing. He said I couldn't go in and look around. "Tell me what you're looking for," he said. I made something up, like, "The Grapes of Wrath." He put his head down, ready to get back to his paper, and said, "I don't got it." I tried a few more titles, but his negative response came more quickly each time, in the last instance before he could possibly have known what book I was asking for.

That was a first: a store owner who didn't want you, or me, at any rate, in his store under any circumstances. Was it a front for some illegal operation? Did the guy really have his merchandise memorized and was just trying to help? Was he stark-raving mad? I settled on stark-raving mad. I confirmed it a couple of other times over the years, getting no further either time, and when I went back for the last time, I think in the late 1980s, the store was gone.

The chances of his having anything worth a damn were slim, but it galled me that I never got a chance to browse. I suppose I could have broken in after hours, but that seemed a little extreme, or tried showing the guy some money or attempted to get a court order on the grounds that the proprietor was discriminating against persons of German-American heritage, but I let it go.

There were things I was not willing to do to satisfy my craving for used books. I would not pay the outlandish prices demanded by an eccentric, nor challenge the dominion of an apparent mad man. But to overcome the terror of a ferocious dog, not once but twice, to take myself up a steep flight of stairs not knowing if I would ever come down?

I could do that, and I might even do it again.

Previously unpublished

GEORGE OSTWALD:
AT PEACE IN HIS PLACE

I met George Ostwald when he took me and the subject of another story up and down his stretch of the Yellowstone River in a jet boat. As the afternoon wore on, I became more interested in Ostwald than in the story I was working on. As he spoke, and as he demonstrated his great love and knowledge of the river, I told myself I should come back someday and do a story about him.

It took a few years, but I finally got around to it, and I was able to spend another fine day on the river with George and then write a profile of him. Toward the end of it, I wrote this:

There is something appealing about traveling widely, getting to know other cultures, peoples and landscapes. But there is something attractive, too, about the idea of getting to know one tiny sliver of the planet extremely well, as Ostwald has done.

When I wrote that, I was thinking of Gregory Frazier, the globe-circling motorcyclist from Fort Smith, whose profile you will find just after this one. Ostwald and Frazier represent the two poles of experience — the man who has been everywhere and seen everything, and the man who has stayed put and become intimately familiar with one small part of the world.

As different as they are, I thought they would have understood each other immediately. They are both adventurers, each experiencing the world in a way that is completely foreign to most of us.

NEAR COLUMBUS — From the deck of George Ostwald's house three miles east of Columbus, it's not exactly a stone's throw to the Yellowstone River, but it's close.

You could throw a rock as far as the railroad tracks, and from the tracks you could toss a rock underhand into the river. Ostwald has been that close to the Yellowstone for most of his 43 years, and he seems to be familiar with every inch of his stretch of the river.

That would be the stretch from a little below Columbus to Park City, about 20 miles. Over the years, Ostwald has swum in it, waded it, inner-tubed on it, navigated it by canoe, raft and jet boat, walked up and down its banks. He has fished every tributary in those 20 miles, investigated every ravine and gully. He has hunted game on its banks, run trap lines, explored its environs for human and natural artifacts.

Nine years ago, he was even married on it. The ceremony took place in his 22-foot canoe — he said "it looks like a Viking ship when it's on the water" — a few miles downstream from his place, at a striking bend in the river where a thick sandstone ledge hangs far out over the water. Ostwald and his wife, Nicole, stood up front near the preacher, with a maid of honor and best man astern of them.

"And my brother in back, just kind of keeping the canoe straight," Ostwald said.

Ostwald was born in Columbus, but his family moved around the state some before settling down near the river when he was in the fourth grade. The family was living on a farm owned by Myron and Emma Langstaff, where Hensley Creek enters the Yellowstone from the north.

That's when Ostwald began to get to know the river.

"I liked to leave early in the morning and spend my day on the river instead of bothering my mom and dad," he said. He'd fish up and down both sides of the river, dropping a line in the main channel or into the creeks and springs that dumped into the Yellowstone. That's also when he began running trap lines, snaring beavers, foxes, raccoons, coyotes and more.

"That kept me out of school a lot at the time," he said. "I was always wanting to check my traps."

In 1980, when he was in the eighth grade, his parents bought their own piece of land a little bit upstream of Hensley Creek, right off old Highway 10, looking down on the railroad tracks and the river. Ostwald and his father and brothers built a two-story house with material salvaged from the railroad roundhouse in Laurel, which was being demolished that year.

He has been there ever since, living on the ground floor with his own family until two years ago, when his parents became traveling retirees and Ostwald bought the house from them.

Ostwald said he ended up with the house because all of his siblings — he had two brothers and three sisters — moved elsewhere "and I was the only one interested." He figures he made the right decision.

"You couldn't replace a piece of property like this anymore," he said.

It includes four acres of land, and Ostwald leases a mile of riverfront from the railroad. He sometimes plants a few small garden patches on the railroad land, but mostly he leases it to guarantee access to the river near his house. And knowing most of the other farmers, ranchers and property owners in the area, he is welcome on much of the river bottom between Park City and Columbus.

Ostwald and his wife have four daughters and one son, ranging in age from 2 to 11, and much of his time on the river these days is spent in their company. Just as he did as a boy, the kids fish and swim, build forts and explore the river. Sometimes he'll take the lot of them down to a nearby island and give them the run of the place. They'll keep themselves busy most of the day.

"I want to raise my kids to respect what they have in front of them and not take it for granted," Ostwald said. "Someday to find work they might have to go to a big city."

It's a possibility that makes Ostwald shiver. For him, Billings is too big, "and every year people are driving crazier and crazier." He went into Billings on an errand recently and realized he hadn't been there in four or five months.

Ostwald's career as miner gives him a lot of long stretches of time to spend in what he calls his "big backyard." During a six-year stint at the Stillwater Mine, he worked a seven-days-on, seven-days-off schedule. For the past eight months or so he has been working as a contract miner in Wallace, Idaho, cycling through a 28-day work schedule that gives him two weeks off at the end of each cycle.

Ostwald said he mostly canoes in the fall and winter, when the river is low, rafts during high water in the spring and uses his jet boat during the summer. He'll go out in any conditions, skimming over barbed-wire fences during floods or snaking down an open channel when the river is mostly iced over. He said it's a thrill to paddle between high walls of blue ice, like floating through a glacier.

At least twice a year, he takes his family and friends and an assortment of watercraft and runs the Yellowstone from Livingston to Laurel. In an average year, he said, he probably puts in at least 1,000 miles on the river.

That doesn't include the time spent walking up and down its banks. He harvests wild asparagus, cuts downed cottonwoods for firewood and sometimes finds beehives thick with honeycombs. He still likes to fish, though many of the old tributaries don't run year-round anymore and don't carry any fish.

After all these years, Ostwald still enjoys exploring the area. He figures he has been up into every ravine on his stretch of river, and sometimes he gets the feeling that he's the first person ever to penetrate some of them, or at least the first in a very long time.

He has a few favorite spots. There's the top of Young's Point, just upstream of Park City, where a rampart of sandstone soars straight up from the river, and there's a bluff near his house where he likes to settle in amid a few ancient tepee rings.

"I like to sit and let my mind drift back a couple hundred years," he said.

He has stumbled onto old graves, of Indians and whites, and he doesn't disturb them. He has collected artifacts that work their way up to the surface, like old French trade beads, corked bottles and marbles, and he has found a few stone mauls. One prize find was a well-preserved bison skull that he dug out of the river bank. It was so old it was partially petrified.

Most of the artifacts he runs across are of more recent vintage. He has found guns, fishing rods, coolers, clothes, even canoes. He has seen bears and bobcats, mule deer and whitetail deer, elk, coons, beavers, skunks, weasels, badgers, otters, minks. Recently he watched a bald eagle battling a goose. The goose finally ran out of steam and the eagle stood over it, pinning its wings to the ground — "just like a wrestler" — before eating it, starting with the neck.

There is something appealing about traveling widely, getting to know other cultures, peoples and landscapes. But there is something attractive, too, about the idea of getting to know one tiny sliver of the planet extremely well, as Ostwald has done.

And because the Yellowstone is an undammed river, it has rewarded Ostwald's devotion with endless delights and a constantly changing appearance. Every spring runoff does something to alter the river's many channels. New gravel bars appear overnight, and old trees are toppled and swept away. The big flood of 1996 created new islands, destroyed a set of rapids that kayakers used to love near Ostwald's house and transformed an island across the river from his place into an extension of the south bank.

The flood also seeded that whole stretch of riverbank with cottonwood trees, which are already some 20 feet high and this time of year blazing with fall colors.

Ostwald said his appreciation of the river only deepens with time. He takes care of his river by always picking up trash left by other people, and he has taught his children to do the same. He welcomes the push to build new accesses on the river, "as long as they respect it and take care of it."

A few years back, Ostwald tried to capitalize on his familiarity with the river by starting a guide service on the Yellowstone. It didn't quite work out.

"I had a hard time charging people," he said. "I'd take them out and they'd ask what they owed, and I'd tell them, 'Really, nothing. If you're enjoying it as much as I am, just do it.' "

Originally published September 29, 2007, in The Billings Gazette

GREGORY FRAZIER:
TAKING ON THE WORLD, AGAIN AND AGAIN

FORT SMITH — The first time Gregory Frazier rode around the world by motorcycle, it took him four years and he wasn't even aware he had done it. Frazier had been motorcycling in various corners of the globe, searching out and filming the best touring roads he could find. He made two videos out of those explorations in the late 1980s, one featuring the 10 best roads in America and another of the top 10 roads in the Alps. In the early '90s, during one of his return trips to the United States, a friend pointed out that Frazier had been completely around the world during his travels, having gone through each of the planet's 24 time zones at least once.

That fired Frazier's ambition, and it was the start of a globe-trotting career that is now unequaled. He is the only person to have ridden solo around the world on a motorcycle four times, and two years ago he went around the world again, this time with a passenger riding behind him. And for Frazier, adventure touring really has become a career. For 20 years he has been riding and racing motorcycles all over the world, and when he's not riding he's writing books and magazine articles, producing videos, leading paid tours or giving presentations on his travels. It hasn't made him wealthy — home base is a single-wide trailer in Fort Smith — but it's all Frazier wants to do.

"I have this disease," he said. "It's called wanderlust. I can't remember not having it."

Darwin Holmstrom, a senior editor with Motorbooks, a publisher of automotive and motorcycle books, commissioned Frazier to write "Motorcycle Touring: Everything You Need to Know," one of at least 10 books Frazier has written.

"I really didn't think of anybody else," Holmstrom said. "He was my first choice."

Holmstrom said he couldn't release sales figures for the book, published in 2005, but called it possibly the best-selling motorcycle touring book ever published. Through the many books and videos, Holmstrom added, Frazier has almost single-handedly created the expanding craze for adventure touring and global motorcycling.

If Frazier, who turned 60 this month, had merely gone around the world by the most direct route, that would be one thing. The shortest route, through the United States, Europe and Russia, involves about 16,000 miles by land. On two of his circumnavigations, Frazier's path traced a huge "W" on the globe, riding up and down the Americas, Europe and Africa to the northernmost and southernmost points on those continents. Along the way he has put more than a million miles on dozens of motorcycles.

Bob Clement, a BMW mechanic whose shop in Roberts, Bob's Motorwerks, is something of a legend among BMW motorcycle owners, has known Frazier for years and knows his place in motorcycling lore. He compared him to the first man to sail around the world.

"Lots of people took off and did what Magellan did, but Magellan did it first," he said. "Greg's the man."

Frazier was born in 1947 in Indiana, where his parents — his father was half-Crow and half-Sioux and his mother was white — were attending a Quaker college. Frazier contracted his infatuation for motorcycles in the early 1960s, after his family moved to Billings. His friend had purchased a 50cc Moped and Frazier wanted one, too. His mother said no, absolutely not, and when he was 15, figuring he needed to get away from things like friends with motorcycles, Frazier's parents sent him off to a Quaker high school in Pennsylvania. It was a mixed success.

"I had to fight my way through Quaker school," Frazier said. "Everyone wanted to take me on. I was the only Indian in the whole school."

At 18, while attending a Quaker college in Philadelphia, Frazier was finally old enough to buy a motorcycle without his mother's permission. His first bike was a Honda 305.

"I rode that thing — I rode it into the ground," he said. "It was just freedom."

In 1970, when he was still in college, he spent a month and a half motorcycling around Europe. It wasn't a major adventure, compared with his later exploits, but it taught him that language was no great barrier and that he could make his way across borders, dealing with visas, paperwork and different currencies.

"After that, the world was mine," he said.

After discovering that he had accidentally circumnavigated the world, Frazier set his sights on a more methodical repeat. He talked to a German travel writer and people at Guinness World Records and was advised to file a formal "flight plan" to document and validate his journey. But Frazier, ever the lone wolf, didn't like the idea of living by anybody else's rules. As for Guinness, he said, "They're in the business of selling books. They'll put you in their book for shoving nails up your nose."

For his second trip, begun in 1997, Frazier decided to trace that giant "W" on the globe, going to the ends of the road on four continents. Those outposts have suitably exotic names: Deadhorse, Alaska; Ushuaia, Argentina; North Cape, Norway; and Cape Agulhaus, South Africa. It took him two years to complete that circumnavigation, including the six months he spent back in the states after running out of money in Africa and flying home to earn enough to complete the trip. He did the whole trek on a 1981 800cc BMW. Although Frazier is a certified BMW mechanic and used to race BMWs, he calls himself a "motorcycle agnostic."

In one of his books, "Riding the World," he said that when people ask him to name the best bike for circling the globe, "My answer is always the same, 'Whichever bike suits you.' "

That willingness to ride almost anything became the basis for his third big trip, begun in 2001. His goal was to ride around the world on motorcycles made on each continent. He soon learned that no bikes were manufactured in Australia, Antarctica or Africa, but he still climbed aboard lots of different machines. Those included a Harley-Davidson and an Indian in the United States, a BMW in Europe and an Enfield, SYN, Hartford and Honda in Asia. In South America, he rode an Amazonas, the only motorcycle ever manufactured there. At the time it was built, the Amazonas was the biggest bike in the world — basically a Volkswagen engine crammed onto an Indian frame.

After Frazier completed his third global ride, his editors at Motorcycle Consumer News asked him to write a series of articles on preparing an unfamiliar motorcycle for a trip around the world. He spent the next six months customizing a Kawasaki KLR 650cc bike with $3,000 worth of improvements. Then came a challenge from a friend. The motorcycle might look primed for a trip around the world, he told Frazier, but how would he know all the modifications were up to the task unless he put the bike to the test? That sliver of doubt, once planted, wouldn't give Frazier any peace, and in 2002 he set off again.

This time he followed a fairly direct route — though with detours to Cuba and the Sahara Desert — spending five months motoring through Europe, across all eight of Russia's time zones and then the United States. Frazier wasn't sure if anyone else had soloed around the world three times by motorcycle, but he knew four times was a singular achievement.

"I was done," he said. "I'd done everything I could think of. I was retired."

Or so he thought. Then Donna-Rae Polk asked him to take her around the world. This was in 2004, a couple of years after Frazier had met Polk in Denver. She was 61 and had been diagnosed with Parkinson's disease. She wanted to go on a dream trip, to see the world before it was too late.

"I said, 'No, honey, I'm done,' " Frazier recalled, but Polk was persistent. He did finally agree to take her, though she was going to have to pay for the trip, and they jointly decided to do another ends-of-the-earth voyage, going as far north and south as they could on four continents.

For all his travels, Frazier has had surprisingly few bad wrecks or injuries. The worst was in Australia, where he smashed into a rock with his foot, breaking his big toe and second toe. His foot got infected and almost had to be amputated. In Brazil, riding up a steep, muddy road in the jungle, he slid backward and then down a ravine into the jungle, with his motorcycle on top of him. He wasn't badly hurt but did lose consciousness, and when he woke up a couple of truck drivers were trying to pull his pants off, apparently to get at his wallet. They weren't thieves, Frazier said, they just thought he was dead. When he woke up, they helped him get his bike back on the road and insisted he spend the night with their families.

He was jailed once in Honduras, after a cop tried to seize one of his two cameras. Frazier attempted to grab his camera back after the cop took it, and when the officer fell to the ground he pulled out his gun, which Frazier said he snatched on impulse, in self-defense. He ended up spending the night in jail, but when the cop's superior saw Frazier's Crow tribal enrollment card, Frazier said, he told the cop it was OK that Frazier took his gun "because he was a great Indian warrior."

"That and $260 — for insulting a police officer — got me out of jail," Frazier said.

On the border between Thailand and Myanmar (formerly Burma), Frazier thought he was being shot at, but he learned later that he happened to be in the middle of a shootout between government and rebel troops. In Philadelphia, he really was shot at, and one bullet pierced the windscreen on his motorcycle.

Frazier's favorite roads are in the Swiss Alps. His least favorite are in China and India. "China might be worse in terms of application of rules, but in India I saw more death on the road than anywhere in the world," he said. In India, the biggest vehicle owns the road, and people will intentionally force smaller vehicles off to the side. Frazier said he got in four accidents, none serious but all frightening, on his first day in India.

He's run into dogs, run over snakes, fixed dozens of flat tires, been stuck in sand, mud and water, contracted malaria, dealt with corrupt customs officials and gotten sick on bad food and water innumerable times. In Morocco, he said, "I met every one of Ali Baba's 40 thieves."

Along the way, he has learned a lot of tricks for staying healthy, staying in motion and staying alive. He never talks politics on the road and always carries some cash. It's unsafe and uninsured, but in a pinch, there's nothing like a wad of cash, he said. For his lifestyle, he needs about $2,000 a month on the road. Frazier has learned a lot about the intricacies of shipping motorcycles around the world, but he also found out it makes more sense to keep most of his 30 or 40 bikes stored all over the world.

"I learned a long time ago to stash motorcycles," he said. "It's cheaper than to ship them all over the planet."

He always wears a helmet, doesn't drive after drinking and keeps his insurance up. He can say "beer" and "toilet" in 24 languages. Fortunately, English is spoken just about everywhere, he said, and sign language will do the trick if nobody speaks English. He was married once — "10 years, eight to 10 years, somewhere in there" — but he's a confirmed bachelor now, in love with the road.

Home base for the past 25 years has been Fort Smith on the Crow Indian Reservation. He has a black single-wide trailer partially enclosed by a black fence festooned with cow skulls. Out front is a black school bus, which he lived in for a couple of years when he was traveling around the country racing motorcycles. Winter's tough in Fort Smith, but he loves it in all seasons.

For this world traveler, there's no place like home.

Originally published September 16, 2007, in The Billings Gazette

A MAN'S SALE

The ad in The Billings Gazette classified section said it all: "MAN'S GARAGE SALE misc. tools, shovels, axes, reloading equip. NO BABY CLOTHES."

Sure enough, Art Veatch's garage sale at 643 St. Johns Ave. was a manly affair.

Makeshift tables were loaded with extension cords, rusty hammers, kerosene lanterns, pickaxes, shears, saws, spades, hair clippers, rat traps, a monkey wrench, fishing rods, tackle boxes, waders, fire extinguishers, a whetstone, an old stove, an electric sander, cigar boxes jammed with nuts and bolts, and four un-opened cans of cooling system conditioner.

And not a scrap of baby clothes in sight.

Veatch, a retired firefighter, said he worded the ad the way he did because he's a dedicated garage sale shopper himself, and there's nothing he hates worse than going to what's advertised as a "huge sale" and finding nothing but mountains of baby clothes.

"This is a man's sale," he said. "I wanted to make that as clear as possible."

Despite the wording of the ad, he said, "We're getting a few women, but not too many."

There was, for the record, one table containing items that

could not be described as entirely masculine. On it were dishes, a few necklaces, a little heart-shaped box adorned with flowers and a glass napkin holder, very bright orange, in the shape of an owl.

Those were the remnants of a failed marriage, Veatch said, the sooner sold and the less said the better. A few minutes later, Joanne Best walked up and made a beeline for the napkin holder, which she bought. She hadn't seen the ad, she said; she was just driving by and noticed the sale.

"I've got one just like it," Best said, cradling the glass owl. "I used it as a bill holder. Except mine wasn't as bright."

Merv Gravos was much more typical of the people stopping by Veatch's sale Friday morning. He purchased a cast-iron skillet, two ice picks, a rusty ax head and an antique slotted shovel used for sifting coals from hot ashes.

He wasn't quite sure he wanted to spend a dollar on the shovel, however, because there was a small crack in the blade. But this was a man's sale, so Veatch grabbed the shovel, strode into his garage, slipped on a mask and welded the shovel back into usable condition, all in a matter of minutes.

"Thanks, guys," Gravos said, gathering up his purchases. "I'm out of money."

Veatch's sale also featured a rusty and seemingly useless collection of battered can and bottle openers, all strung together on a corroded piece of wire. It was purchased by a Gazette photographer and a reporter, who were, after all, men.

They went halves on the sticker price of one buck.

Originally published August 28, 1998, in The Billings Gazette

EVEL KNIEVEL, R.I.P.

BUTTE — Evel Knievel's family said it wanted his memorial service to be a celebration of his life, but it felt as much like a celebration of Butte.

For better or worse, they just don't make characters in Billings, or in Bozeman, Missoula, Helena or Great Falls, like they do in Butte, at least not any more.

Characters like Bob Kovacich, an old friend of Knievel's, who was decked out for the funeral in a dapper suit, vest and classic fedora. But what really caught my eye were the massive rings, one on each finger. Two of them were gifts from Evel, one a heavy gold thing with an inlaid diamond-studded "K," the other with a little figure of Evel, outlined in tiny diamonds, jumping his motorcycle. Did I mention that Kovacich also had a diamond stud in one of his front teeth and another in his left ear lobe?

At one point Kovacich was standing with 10 or 12 other men who knew Knievel well. There were gold chains, a few deep tans, expensive haircuts and well-tailored suits. It looked like a gathering of extras for one of the "Godfather" movies.

Sitting by himself on the bleachers in the back of the Butte Civic Center, wearing a black top hat with blue feather plumes, was Rudi Giecek. He owns the Dumas Brothel, which he converted into a museum years ago before the enterprise went bust. He's hoping to reopen the museum this summer.

Giecek said he thinks he was the first person ever to film a Knievel stunt. He was just a kid then and walked five miles from Meaderville, a Butte enclave later swallowed by the Berkeley Pit, to the Butana Speedway. Evel's stunt was roaring once around the track on his motorcycle and smashing through a wooden outhouse.

"He put his head down and went straight through it," Giecek said, and he got it all on 8mm film, which he still has in his possession.

Elsewhere in the Civic Center was 8-year-old Keanan Fitzpatrick, wearing a wee replica of Knievel's trademark star-spangled jumpsuit and cape, handmade by his grandmother. And like Knievel's costume, it had the lucky rabbit's foot attached to the zipper, sort of.

"We couldn't find a bunny tail, so we just made our own," Keanan said.

Another pal of Knievel's, Spanky Spangler, spoke at a press conference before the service, squeezed in between appearances by the Rev. Robert Schuller, the televangelist, and Smokin' Joe Frazier, the boxer. Spanky recalled that Evel, sitting in a bar in Vegas, pointed out the window to a guy lying in a lawn chair by the pool. Evel suggested going out to the pool and throwing him in the water. People didn't usually veto Evel's ideas, so they went out and dumped the guy into the pool. Turned out he was asleep and could barely swim, and when Evel ran off, Spanky felt obligated to jump in and help the guy.

"He was so fun," Spanky said of Knievel. "Kinda reckless, but fun."

Gene Sage remembered playing hockey with Knievel. There were eight teams in Butte back then, in the late 1950s, and Sage played on an all-star team with Knievel. He played left wing with Knievel, a center, and he recalled how in high school, before hockey sticks with curved blades were developed, they'd skip school, get into the Civic Center with the connivance of the manager and practice lifting the puck — sending it airborne on a shot.

Pucks weren't the only thing Knievel wanted to get airborne.

Sage talked about going to the Beef Trail ski area with Knievel and sneaking onto the intermediate jump, soaring off it on pitch-dark nights. He thinks that's maybe where Knievel got the idea of jumping motorcycles.

Sunday night, when photographer David Grubbs and I were in the Met Tavern, talking to people who knew Knievel, it became almost overwhelming. There were too many people with too many good stories. We couldn't talk to them all, and we had to pass up yarns we would have killed for on a regular story.

But the passing of Evel Knievel was no regular story, and Butte has never been a regular town. It was nice to be reminded at the funeral of this larger-than-life character that his hometown still harbors so many other characters.

Maybe that was the key to Evel's success. If you had enough talent and guts to make your mark in Butte, taking on the rest of the world was a snap.

Originally published December 11, 2007, in The Billings Gazette

EVEL KNIEVEL, THE AFTERMATH

BUTTE — It's not easy covering Evel Knievel, even when he's dead. I went over to Butte with photographer David Grubbs to cover Knievel's funeral, which was on a cold, cold Monday in mid-December. I wrote a couple of stories Sunday and then attended Knievel's surreal sendoff at the Civic Center the next day.

I wrote a couple more stories in the Montana Standard newsroom — which sent me back more than 25 years to the start of my career — and had them shipped over to Billings by 6 p.m. Grubbs and I went out for dinner with some newspaper friends from Butte and then, about 7:30, set off on our own to see if we could find any of Knievel's friends and associates still out and about.

Our first stop was the Met Tavern, across the street from the Civic Center, where we had found so many great characters the night before, but it was nearly deserted. The bartender said he could hardly believe it, either. So we made our way to the M&M, which was a bit more lively, but only because seven or eight coeds from Montana Tech, accompanied by their professor in the nursing department, were celebrating the end of the semester. It was mildly interesting to watch them dancing and singing along with the jukebox at the top of their lungs, but impromptu karaoke was not what we were after.

I didn't know where else to go, figuring maybe everyone had done their carousing Sunday night and were all through. So I told Grubbs we should at least go down to one of my favorite bars, the Silver Dollar, before heading back to our room in the Finlen Hotel. But then it occurred to me that I should also give Grubbs a quick tour of the Pekin Noodle Parlor, just up the street from the Silver Dollar. Grubbs is a native of Helena and I thought he had been insufficiently appreciative of Butte's ragged charms. The Pekin rarely fails to impress people, what with its long, steep set of stairs and its row of little wood-paneled booths, each with its own pink curtain. I also wanted to show him the kitchen, which has a couple of gigantic woks and looks like the kind of place you might have seen in San Francisco a century ago.

So we walked up the stairs, opened the door — and the first person we saw, making her way down the center aisle between the booths, was Krystal Knievel, Evel's widow. She ducked into a booth and pulled the curtain.

I turned to Grubbs and said, "I think we may have hit the jackpot."

I figured we had plenty of time, so I told Grubbs I still wanted him to see the kitchen before we did any more exploring. The Pekin proprietor, Danny, graciously showed off his woks and other accoutrements, talking rapidly all the while. I don't know why it's always so thrilling to look at that kitchen and talk to Danny, but Grubbs was starting to get a look of stunned wonderment on his face, which was all I had hoped for.

That done, we walked to the other end of the restaurant, to a small banquet room, to find it crammed with Knievel family members, friends, hangers-on and bodyguards. I recognized and said hello to the Rev. Gene Sullivan, who had worked for Knievel years ago, broke with him and started his own "Jump for Jesus" motorcycle ministry in Billings. I had written about him in the late 1990s, just before he took his whole show to Tonga, invited there by the king of Tonga. At the funeral, Sullivan told of how he reconciled with Knievel, who had found Jesus not long before his death.

Anyway, Grubbs and I soon realized that we were the only customers in the Pekin who were not part of the gang. Nobody seemed to mind our presence, not even those who knew we were journalists from earlier encounters. But we had left our tools of the trade behind and we were off the clock, just interested in soaking in the whole weird scene.

Speaking of soaking, we soon shuffled into the tiny little Pekin bar attached to the banquet room, where the loudest person by far was a baby-face fellow in a black leather motorcycle jacket who insisted on buying rounds of drinks and was noisily knocking back shots of Jack Daniels. We couldn't make out who he was, but he kept shouting out little snatches of praise for Evel Knievel, or boasting of some kind of stunt he was contemplating, all in an Australian accent.

The bar finally quieted down when the local news came on and we all watched 10 minutes' worth of coverage of the funeral. I was mostly watching Krystal, noting her reactions. She looked wistful when excerpts of Robbie Knievel's funeral oration were aired, but when he ended with a roar, "I am not the greatest daredevil in the world! I am the son of the greatest daredevil in the world!" she and everyone else in the bar erupted with shouts and cheers. And when Matthew McConaughey delivered his line about Evel flying forever up in Heaven, Krystal smiled and slowly nodded her head.

After that Grubbs and I wandered around a bit, from the bar to the banquet room and then to various booths, listening in on and sometimes joining conversations. At one point we found ourselves in the aisle between the booths, standing there with the Australian kid, who by now looked hardly able to stand. He introduced himself as Robbie Maddison, a daredevil motorcycle stuntman from Sydney, Australia, who was going to set a world's record for the longest motorcycle jump ever, on New Year's Eve, live on ESPN. He told us to check out his Web site and he showed us his scars, including a long one on his left arm — "I broke my arm in the same place Evel did!" — and several more on his abdomen. He also had the unsettling habit of lowering his retainer, and his two front teeth, with his tongue, to show the gap in his choppers.

A bit later, another guy in a motorcycle jacket came rolling out of the banquet room in a wheelchair and asked for help getting down the Pekin's enormous flight of stairs. There were three other fellows at hand, so I made a fourth, grabbing his wheelchair by the left rear handle. After we slowly and safely got him down to street level, I asked him, "So, who are you?" The other guys who had been helping carry him began talking all at once, shouting out something about the guy being one of the greatest daredevils ever, the godfather of stunt riding, Evel's inspiration and God knows what else. He told me his name was Bob Gill and that I should check out *his* Web site. I said I would.

Back up in the bar, Robbie Maddison was getting even drunker, which I shouldn't have thought possible, and considerably wilder. He was also buying more drinks. Twice I tried to buy a round for me and Grubbs, but the bartender pointed to a couple of Heinekens on the bar and said, "Take those. Robbie already paid for them." A bit later, Maddison's friends apparently decided he'd had enough and they tried to talk him into leaving. When he said no, they resorted to force, with one beefy guy in black grabbing him around the chest and dragging him through the door. Maddison braced his arms against the door frame, whacking me in the jaw in the process, causing me to bite my tongue. He kept shouting, in his slurred Aussie accent, "Leave me alone! Put me down! Have some fooking respect, man!" They finally dragged him down the stairs and out.

Toward the end of our little soiree, I found myself talking to Jimmy Dick, one of my favorite characters of the past two days. He used to work for Evel, but neither he nor his friends would ever say exactly what he did. When I asked, they all burst into laughter, leaving things to my imagination. Jimmy is a square-jawed, devilishly handsome fellow, very cheerful and all smiles, but you got the impression he could swing into action, and get very angry, at a moment's notice. A guy sitting next to him, last name of Harrington, knew I was a reporter and he told me not to say anything bad about Butte. I told him I wouldn't dream of it, and I repeated to him some of the things I had written the day before, about Butte being so rich in characters. He seemed to think I was all right.

Things wound down pretty quickly after Maddison's departure. There were platters of food and the remains of food everywhere, empty cans and bottles and cigarette butts, and lots of people giving their last hugs goodbye or shaking hands.

Grubbs and I went down to the Silver Dollar for that one

beer we had planned to have two or three hours earlier, then walked up to the Finlen to get some sleep. Grubbs decided to get one more beer to take up to the room, so we ducked into the Finlen bar off the lobby. Who should we see on entering the joint but Robbie Maddison and his whole crew, and by now Robbie was almost uncontrollable. When Grubbs got his beer, Robbie suddenly lunged at him and tried to grab it. There was some shouting and scuffling, but Grubbs emerged with his drink and we made our way upstairs, laughing at all the strange adventures we'd had.

I can't imagine why Grubbs didn't think to say anything at the time, but it wasn't until the next morning, when he woke up, that he sat up in his bed and said, "Damn! That guy bit me on the arm."

"Who did?" I asked.

"That crazy Australian daredevil," he said. Yep, during the brief scuffle, Robbie Maddison, the heir of Evel Knievel, the amazing stuntman from Australia, had clamped his choppers, fake teeth and all, on Grubbs' left arm. Luckily, Grubbs was wearing a sweater and a jacket, so not much harm was done.

And in a city bursting with great stories, Grubbs now had his own. I have to admit, I was a little bit jealous.

Originally published December 12, 2007, in the City Lights blog

MOUNTAIN MAN:
LIFE ON HIS OWN TERMS

Back in the mid-1970s, I went with a group of friends to a place just outside the western edge of Glacier National Park, where the parents of one of our party owned some land. There were four or five cabins on the property, tended by a caretaker who lived there year round.

This caretaker dressed in handmade buckskin clothes, wore a fur cap and leather leggings, sported a black beard and rarely ventured out even for a walk in the woods without a rifle and a couple of big knives. He ran trap lines, killed his own meat, tanned hides, did scrimshaw on elk antlers and kept a spacious root cellar. It was stocked with everything from canned fruit and vegetables to smoked hams, which hung from the cellar's big hand-hewn roof beams.

He amazed us all by starting a fire with a flint and a steel striker, using wood so damp I'm not sure I could have done the job with matches and gasoline. To my inexperienced eye, he looked every inch the mountain man, strong, content and independent. It seemed to be a pretty good life.

You didn't have to be around him for more than a couple of hours, though, before you realized there was a serpent in the garden. He wasn't there just to enjoy nature's bounty and a life of freedom.

He was convinced that the United States, within a few years at most, would be plunged into chaos and civil war. When that day came, he told us, running his index finger slowly across his throat, he intended to settle a few scores down in the flatlands. That done, he would retreat to his northern stronghold — and God help anyone who thought he intended to share his food.

I had never met anyone like him at the time, but in the years since then I've learned that he was merely a prototype of the kind of person that many of our fellow Americans now picture when they think of the word "Montanan." Of course the characterization is unfair, but I will say this for the mountain man: He is a better representative of the state than the people who created that national image — the Freemen, the Unabomber, the Militia of Montana folks and the assorted racists and separatists we've all become so familiar with.

The mountain man never attempted to impose his views on the rest of the world. We came to learn of his unsavory plans for the future only because we intruded on his solitude and asked prying questions.

The Unabomber, by contrast, was not content to sit in his anchorite's shack ruminating on his hatred of civilization. He actively put his hatred to work, mailing out bombs, killing people, demanding that newspapers publish his Russian-novel-size manifesto. The Freemen also imposed themselves on the world, in a big way. They manufactured bogus money orders and other financial "instruments," hoping simultaneously to strike it rich and to paralyze financial institutions and government agencies.

The Militia of Montana was even more crass. Its mission, aside from granting interviews with reporters from around the world, was to sell products tied to its anti-government, anti-establishment themes — books, clothing, food, medical supplies, gas masks and other survival gear, more or a less a boutique of far-right baubles.

Our mountain man indulged in nothing of the kind. He sat up on the border like a backwoods Robinson Crusoe, isolated, self-sufficient and above all private. He was just another crank who wanted to be left alone, a desire people in these parts are famously willing to oblige. From the early days, when ex-Confederates made their way to Montana Territory to escape the humiliation of Reconstruction, to the much later influx of movie stars who just wanted to enjoy their million-dollar cottages in peace, Montana has been big enough for everybody.

The unspoken compact was broken when some of the cranks began seeking converts. The Freemen trolled for disciples all across the country, and the Militia of Montana maintained a Web site as slick as a camo rain poncho.

Theodore Kaczynski could have lived peacefully in Lincoln for the rest of his life, but he got it into his head that his daring acts — mailing out bombs — and his dizzying intellect, distilled into his manifesto, would bring the modern world to its knees.

My memories of the mountain man, as wild and extreme as he appeared when I was introduced to him, grow milder every year, until he seems almost quaint. A delusional hermit living deep in the hinterlands of Montana, unknown to the world, undisturbed, unindicted — those were the days.

Originally published March 19, 2000, in The Billings Gazette

READING MONTANA

I can't imagine what my uncle must have thought when I called him from the University of Montana in Missoula in the winter of 1974 and told him I was going to be living in the woods that coming spring. I'm from Minnesota, and during high school I lived with my aunt and uncle in a suburb of Minneapolis. Most of our clan who had left Minnesota had stayed in the Midwest or had gone off to the East Coast. I chose Montana, for reasons that included a bit of romanticism, a little hearsay and for the most part a heedless whimsy, which I was big on in those days. And there I was in the second quarter of my first year of college, announcing that I was going to be living outside, or nearly so. My friend from New York and I were going to live in a tent, or possibly under a lean-to. Our plan was to continue our higher education but to live in Hellgate Canyon, the narrow chute through which the Clark Fork River enters Missoula from the east. We planned to settle in about a mile from campus, close enough so we could walk back to civilization every morning handsomely begrimed and smelling of wood smoke.

What, my uncle wanted to know, had inspired my rather unusual resolution? It wasn't something easy to explain.

I am susceptible to the influence of books. When I think of

my childhood I am more apt to picture pages from "A Fly Went By" than actual scenes inhabited by my younger self. The first time I read "The Lord of the Rings" trilogy, I spent much of one summer in Middle Earth, with only occasional forays back to the drab kingdom of Suburbia. Once, reading Thomas Mann's "The Magic Mountain," set in a Swiss sanatorium full of feverish tuberculosis patients, I contracted — or willed myself to develop — a raging, hallucinatory fever, the worst of my life. And during winter quarter of my first year of college, I took a literature class, which I believe was called "Cowboys and Indians: Literature of Red and White." Of the books we read I remember only two, Dan Cushman's "Stay Away, Joe," which was good, and A.B. Guthrie's "The Big Sky," which was more than good. It was transformative, in the sense of having persuaded a citified teenager who possessed no skills or knowledge that would have done him any good in the wilderness to imagine himself a backwoodsman. How could I explain to my uncle that I wanted not merely to live in Montana but to live out, in my own small way, the story of Montana as constructed by A.B. Guthrie?

"The Big Sky" is mainly the story of Boone Caudill, a headstrong young Kentuckian who lights out for the West in 1830 in search of freedom, of unfettered wildness. I was not unmoved by the plot, or by great tragedy at the heart of the book, but what stirred me most at the time were Guthrie's descriptions of the land itself, this "great sprawling magnitude of the west" that I found myself in. I was intoxicated by the grandeur of Guthrie's vision, by scenes like this:

High along the slopes of the peaks the snow lay patched. Between the mountains and the Missouri was high, bare country, where a man on a rise saw buttes swimming in the distance and the distance itself rolling off so far that he lost himself looking into it.

In truth, Missoula was in a tight, hemmed-in valley, and Hellgate Canyon was more compressed still, but this vastly beautiful place was my new home, and Guthrie showed me large parts of it that I could not have found grander had I discovered them on my own.

And of course I responded to the lives of the mountain

men. I wasn't much older than Boone, so the allure of living on my own, out under the stars, answerable to no one, not even to teachers of Western literature, was powerfully attractive. My friend from New York, after reading the book at my urging, fell just as hard for it. We wanted to be Boone Caudill and his friends Jim Deakins and Dick Summers. In the afternoon, after our classes were over, we'd leave our dorm rooms in Duniway Hall and tramp up Hellgate Canyon. We'd build a fire in a swale not far from the river and sit there drinking quart bottles of Lucky Lager, smoking hand-rolled cigarettes and palavering in our best imitation of our new heroes, larding our speech with "I reckon," "this child" and "I'm thinkin.' " It was during those afternoons that we cooked up our plans to live outside. We both realized it was all a bit silly, but we didn't care. What did the people we passed our days with, mere students, know about the melancholic fatality the wide-open West engendered in thoughtful mountain men like Deakins:

The feel of the country settled into Jim, the great emptiness and age of it, the feel of westward mountains old as time and plains wide as forever and the blue sky flung across.

The country didn't give a damn about a man or any animal. It let the buffalo and the antelope feed on it and the gophers dig and the birds fly and men crawl around, but what did it care, being one with time itself? What did it care about a man or his hankerings or what happened to him? There would be other men after him and others after them, all wondering and all wishful and after a while all dead.

I didn't try explaining all this to my uncle. He had been bewildered but compliant, and had even agreed to let me have the money that ordinarily would have paid for my room and board. I'm sure he was relieved when our plans fell apart. The closer spring quarter got, the sillier the prospect looked. What finally killed it was the impossibility of finding a sufficiently secluded spot within walking distance of campus, for Hellgate Canyon was regularly traversed by numerous other college students, a smattering of older folks and too damned many young kids, who were our main worry. We realized that our camp would be plundered and vandalized if it were anywhere near close enough to walk back and forth to school. We took some ribbing from friends when we gave up on our little dream, but I had no regrets. At 18, life-altering resolutions are as easily abandoned as conceived, and we had an awful lot of fun just imagining ourselves as mountain men.

If I gave up my plans to live like Boone Caudill, I never let go of "The Big Sky." I read it through two or three more times, and for years it was my bedside book, the one I turned to when I wanted to read for a few minutes in the morning, or when I was nodding off at night but not quite ready for sleep. In a sense it speeded up the acclimation process. It filled in some of the missing history and sense of place that people born here would have learned by osmosis. It didn't make me a Montanan — I still haven't figured out how long you have to live here before you feel comfortable hanging that label on yourself — but it went a long way toward making me want to be one.

That didn't prevent my whimsy from luring me back to Minnesota in the mid-1980s. But after five years in the Twin Cities, my wife, a native of Missoula, and I were so eager to move back to Montana that I accepted a job in Billings. In the past, I had never gone to Billings except in the company of the Missoula Flying Mules, a barely organized, nominally adult men's hockey team that played all its games on the road because Missoula in those days didn't have its own rink. Always coming here as an outsider, a challenger, had something to do with the image of Billings I developed, but my dislike for the town went deeper than that. The stink of the place alone — from the oil refineries, the sugar beet plant and a now-defunct meatpacking plant — was enough to make us glad we were just weekend drop-ins. And unlike Missoula, with its loose, late-hippie feel and its large population of college students, Billings seemed to be a collection of arrogant oil men and go-getter business types in spanking-new cowboy hats and freshly ironed blue jeans. But The Billings Gazette had offered me a job as a night editor and Billings was in Montana and that was the main thing.

I had been in Billings barely more than a month, in the summer of 1989, full of doubts and wondering what I'd gotten myself into, when I fell under the sway of another Montana book. I had just read "The California and Oregon Trail" by Francis Parkman, the great historian's account of his ethnographical sortie into the land of the Plains Indians in 1846. It was a fascinating read but marked by a pervasive condescension toward the Indians. That was forgivable, considering when it was written, but I wanted more direct knowledge about Indian life. A friend recommended "Plenty-coups, Chief of the Crows," by Frank Linderman.

Plenty-coups was born in 1848, not far from the present site of Billings. In the late 1920s, nearly blind and not completely trusting his memory, Plenty-coups, aided by interpreters and sign language, sat down and told the story of his life to Linderman. Even in Plenty-coups' youth the lifestyle of the Plains Indians was clearly doomed, but when he brought to life the world he knew as a boy, it was if that world would go on forever. The freedom that Boone Caudill struggled to extract from the West was given to Plenty-coups as a birthright. He had nothing to rebel against or to run from, only a promise to live up to.

"My heart was afire," Plenty-coups told Linderman. "I wished so to help my people, to distinguish myself, so that I might wear an eagle's feather in my hair. How I worked to make my arms strong as a grizzly's, and how much I practiced with my bow! A boy never wished to be a man more than I."

My own heart was afire. It was like reading ancient history, for like the ancient Greeks, Plenty-coups had dedicated himself to honor, harsh pleasures, and war. And like the heroes of the Trojan War, he always spoke in high praise of his vanquished enemies, making sure to point out how handsome and brave his victims had been. The Crow Indians raised their boys in an atmosphere of intense emulation, constantly inspiring them with examples of bravery and endurance. The young boys learned to run by chasing butterflies, which they would catch and rub on their bodies, hoping to obtain their powers. They swam in the rivers at all seasons of the year, dodging ice floes in the winter. When he was a young man, Plenty-coups said, he could run from sunup to sundown without stopping, and you believe him. If there are not so many rapturous descriptions of the land here as in "The Big Sky," it is because they are not necessary. It is a given that there is no finer spot on earth. As another Crow chief, Arapooish, said in a famous speech, "The Crow country is exactly in the right place. Everything good is to be found there. There is no country like the Crow country."

Plenty-coups' book immediately altered the way I looked at Billings. It was no longer a cowtown that had changed into a crass, rough-and-ready commercial burg. Now it had a past and a context that stretched back beyond the edge of written history, and its landmarks seemed full of mystery and meaning. Just as "The Big Sky" had speeded up my internship as a newcomer to Montana, "Plenty-coups" made me love this part of Montana, in just a few days, in a way that I could not have loved it at all without the book. And when I finished it, a friend took me down to Pryor, on the Crow Reservation, to the two-story wooden house where Plenty-coups had lived in his old age. We sat under the same cottonwood trees that shaded Plenty-coups as he dictated the story of his life to Linderman. We peered into his locked and empty house and we even presumed to make tobacco offerings at the little spring-fed pool near his house.

Older if not wiser by then, and having a job and two daughters, I harbored no dreams of going off to live in the mountains. But I couldn't look over the Yellowstone Valley, or off toward the Pryor, Beartooth or Crazy mountains without thinking of Plenty-coups. I took my daughters down to Plenty-coups' house and into the Pryors, and we swam in the Yellowstone River more often than my wife considered altogether prudent. I never quite shook the feeling of strangeness that came over me when I thought of Plenty-coups — the idea that this man who seemed so ancient and inaccessible had lived where I lived, and his house still stood, and he had died only a generation before I was born. I wasn't so fortunate as to have the circle of elders who counseled Plenty-coups when he was a boy and who affirmed the strength of the vision he had high up in the Crazy Mountains, but it seemed to me that books like "The Big Sky" and "Plenty-coups" were our elders, if only we would listen to them.

There were other Montana books that served as elders and that schooled me and moved me over the years. Norman Mac-Lean's "A River Runs Through It," James Welch's "Fools Crow," Richard O'Malley's "Mile High Mile Deep" — all books that had to be read more than once, and which grew on me nearly as much as "Plenty-coups" and "The Big Sky" had done. I haven't lived in enough places or read enough books to hazard an opinion on our relative standing, or even to know whether I sound laughably provincial, but it seems as though Montana is blessed with a disproportionate bounty in terms of natural beauty and the stature of our books.

Which brings me to one more, "We Pointed Them North: Recollections of a Cowpuncher," by E.O. "Teddy Blue" Abbott. Like "Plenty-coups," this is an as-told-to memoir, in this case dictated to and compiled by Helena Huntington Smith. The old cowboy, like the old Crow Chief, didn't need much editing. As Smith says in the introduction, her main job "was to keep out of the way and not mess it up by being literary." It might seem strange that I'm including two ghost-written memoirs among my three favorite pieces of Montana "literature," but here we are in the company of the ancients again, when the best stories were told by people who had lived their adventures, not simply narrated them.

Teddy Blue was born in England in 1860, 12 years after Plenty-coups. He came to the United States in 1871 and settled with his family in Nebraska. Soon after their arrival, Abbott's father bought some cattle in Texas and Teddy Blue was allowed to join the drive to Nebraska, the family thinking it would be good for the health of the "poorliest, sickliest little kid you ever saw," as Teddy Blue described himself. Teddy Blue was soon a bonafide cowpuncher, going all the way from Texas to Montana for the first time in 1883. He tells his story more or less chronologically, but no one ever enjoyed a digression more. And these are not the digressions of a scatter-brained old man. Teddy Blue knew he was telling the story of a heroic group of men that he was proud to be part of, and he wanted to get every detail of their lives down: their gear and their clothing, their grub and their methods of working, their ways of fighting and thinking and taking pleasure. It was a life of incredible hardship and danger, where dismemberment and death awaited the smallest slip. When the cattle were on the move or had to get to water, the cowboys stayed in the saddle so long they would rub tobacco juice in their eyes to keep awake. And it was no use complaining: "If you said anything to the boss, he would only say, 'What the hell are you kicking about? You can sleep all winter when you get to Montana.' " Fat chance. Those cowpunchers were so fired up by the time they hit a wide-open town like Miles City, Montana, that they might have gotten more sleep on the trail.

"I never had time to gamble," Teddy Blue said; "I couldn't sit still long enough; I always had to be up, talking, singing, drinking at the bar. I was so happy and full of life, I used to feel, when I got a little whiskey inside me, that I could jump twenty feet in the air. I'd like to go back and feel that way once more. If I could go back I wouldn't change any of it." The whole book is like that — vivid, unrepentant, electrifyingly alive. I have sometimes thought there might be a connection between extremely difficult, hazardous occupations and the flowering of a language lively and direct enough to encompass them — witness Melville aboard a whaler, or Twain piloting a steamboat. As Smith says of Teddy Blue's English, "of all the varieties of speech in the United States, I don't know any that for color and violence can touch the authentic Western American." I was smitten by his language, and by his evocation of a glorious, fleeting chapter in the history of this state. The plains and rivers of Eastern Montana took on new meaning for me, and Miles City, which I barely knew before reading Teddy Blue, has fascinated me ever since.

In these three books we have the three great themes of early Montana: the twilight of the Plains Indian tradition; the mountain man's glory in that brief era when a European could at least pretend to share in Eden; and that even shorter period when the open-range cowboy was king, when a man lived in the saddle and there wasn't a fence to be seen all the way from Texas to Montana. But these three books that have shaped and re-shaped the way I feel about Montana have more in common than geography, and they describe more than mythological lives. In all of them, there is a feeling of great sadness at the end being near, the curtain coming down. When Plenty-coups was a boy, his powerful vision was of "buffalo without number" coming out of a hole in the ground. When they finally stopped coming, they were all suddenly gone, and then out of the hole came countless more bulls, cows and calves. But these were all spotted buffalo, "strange animals from another world." They were the white man's cattle, which Plenty-coups had not seen before he dreamt of them. It seemed impossible, but come they did, and then the buffalo were gone. Plenty-coups speaks of the transition with a note of noble fatality, only noting, not complaining. In Guthrie's fiction, Boone Caudill makes an attempt to hang onto the vanishing past. He takes a Blackfoot wife and wants nothing more, he thinks, than to live as an Indian, only to realize at the end of "The Big Sky" that he himself had a hand in killing paradise. In real life, Teddy Blue married the half-Snake Indian daughter of Montana pioneer Granville Stuart, and he quotes with approval what his friend, the artist Charlie M. Russell, said of the Indians: "They've been living in heaven for a thousand years, and we took it away from 'em for forty dollars a month."

You want Plenty-coups and Boone Caudill and Teddy Blue Abbott to be 20 years old forever, but it can't happen, even in the pages of a book. And Montana can't just be this beautiful, un-complicated place. As our stories tell us, it is haunted by all the things that cannot be undone.

Originally published in the Winter 2009 issue of Montana Quarterly

KOSTAS:
THE SWEET MYSTERY OF SONG

BELGRADE — Kostas has written hundreds of songs in his life, including more than a few Nashville hits, but he doesn't pretend to understand what makes people connect with a particular song.

"Music is a fluid, instant, combustible, mighty force to reckon with," he says, as when a crowd at a ballpark sings the national anthem, or when churchgoers join their voices on a hymn. But how do you write a song that somebody else wants to sing, and that other people will want to listen to again and again?

"A lot of that I don't understand," Kostas says. "I just call it a sweet mystery."

In the same mysterious way, music wasn't something Kostas consciously decided to do. It was just part of the fabric of growing up in Billings in the late 1950s and early '60s, and before he knew it, it had become his life.

Kostas, an only child, was born in Salonika, in northern Greece, in 1949, and his parents emigrated to the United States when he was 7. Brought to Montana by a sponsor who had also come from Greece, Kostas and his parents lived in Savage for a year and a half before moving to Billings in 1958. By the time he was 9, Kostas was hawking newspapers and shining shoes. It sounds crazy now, but he stayed out until 10 or 11 on weeknights and even later on weekends, walking from his home near North Park to a circuit of bars like the Horseshoe, the Log Cabin, the Carlin, the Mint, the Rainbow and the Mile Away.

Other kids making money the same way had their own regular stops, and there were invariably disagreements over whose turf was whose.

"Fightin' every day, fightin' every night" is the way Kostas describes it, but it paid well. "I came home every day with a pocketful of change," sometimes as much as $15 or $20. He learned early on that he could make more money if he sang while he shined shoes. He sang "On the Wings of a Snow White Dove" and "He's Got the Whole World in His Hands," and the dimes and quarters rolled in.

"Back in those days, Billings was pretty much a rowdy little cow town," Kostas says, and on Saturday afternoons there were taverns that had all-day country-music jam sessions. People started recognizing the little Greek kid with the good voice, and he'd be invited up on stage to sing a song or two. More money came his way, and he started learning about the sweet mystery of the music business.

"Somehow I endeared those people to me. It worked out for both of us."

In those days he was listening to classic country, to the likes of Ernest Tubb and Kitty Wells, Ferlin Husky and Ray Price. But he was also hearing a new kind of music from people like the Everly Brothers and Duane Eddy. Kostas' mother wanted him to take up the accordion, but he talked her into buying him a guitar, a Harmony Sovereign, when he was 9 or 10. He remembers it had thick, heavy strings and a neck like a 2-by-4, but he stuck with it. He had a few basic music lessons early on, but otherwise he was self-taught.

Then came the Beatles and the rest of the musical wave known as the British Invasion. It seemed as though everybody was playing an instrument in those days, and the band scene in Billings exploded. Kostas' first band, in 1964, was called The Leaders. Other bands he formed or joined included Poison Ivy, the Foregone Conclusion, the Fabulous Lost Cause Band, the Bar

Bones, the Sound Establishment, the Jinx (so named because they couldn't find gigs) and Hunger (for much the same reason).

Kostas rattles off dozens of names from those years. People he played with in Billings included guitarists Jerry Grooms, John Uribe, Ronnie Horton, Bob Brown, Jocko Wilcox, Bobby Anderson, Doug Stoughton, Pete Lazetich and Jack Vaughan, bass players Lynn Steinmetz and Dave Frost, drummers Randy McGee and Dev Hutchinson.

Kostas quit school in 1967 during his senior year, having already missed a lot of school when he suffered a detached retina in a fight. He kept playing music through the early 1970s, eventually developing a solo act and performing a mix of covers and his own songs. He says he doesn't really know when he began writing music. Improvisation and invention just seemed to go hand in hand from the first time he sang in public as a young boy.

"In the beginning you emulate, then you imitate, then you create," he says.

In the 1970s, he performed often in Missoula, where he attracted a following with his piercing voice, distinctive guitar style and passionate delivery. By the mid-1980s, though, some of the shine was going out of the music business. Disco was big and live music was becoming scarce and Kostas wasn't getting any younger.

"Hairs were dropping off my head," he says. "I was feeling and noticing a change in my existence." He tried breaking into the music scene in L.A., but nobody there was interested in buying his songs.

His break came when a musician friend, Claire Lynch, who had made it to Nashville in the 1980s, played some of his songs for producer Tony Brown. Brown liked what he heard and arranged for Kostas to sign on as a songwriter for Welk Music. In 1989, Kostas sent in his first batch of 10 songs to Welk.

Brown had Patty Loveless listen to the songs and she ended up using three of them on her 1989 album "Honky Tonk Angel." All three were hits, and "Timber, I'm Falling in Love" went to No. 1 on the country charts. After his long apprenticeship, Kostas was something of an overnight songwriting sensation.

There followed a long succession of Kostas-penned hits for Loveless, Dwight Yoakam, Travis Tritt, Martina McBride, the Dixie Chicks and Holly Dunn, among others. Another No. 1 song he wrote for Loveless, "Blame It on Your Heart," was recognized by BMI as the most performed country song of 1994.

Lonnie Bell, a Billings radio host who was inducted into the Country Music DJ Hall of Fame and who is credited with discovering several country stars, including Loretta Lynn, says Kostas "seems to get along real well with all the insider good musicians."

There's no end of songwriters trying to get heard in Nashville, Bell said, and the trick is getting people to listen. Kostas managed to do that because he's a very good guitar player and singer, and an easy person to talk to.

"They see he's real, is what I'm saying," Bell says.

The year Kostas started writing for Nashville, he also moved to Belgrade, where he bought a two-story building next door to the Mint Bar. He needed the room, having already become quite a collector. He says he started out gathering up old guitars, then old amplifiers and other equipment. Then he began indulging a general passion for antiques, gradually stuffing his building with Western artifacts, curios, collectibles and rare books.

"Everything I like these days is old," he says — and then the songwriter in him kicks in and he adds, "except my women."

His long, many-chambered apartment takes up the top floor, which gives out onto a spacious deck overlooking the alley. The ground floor is home to his store, Old Highway 10 Antiques, which he describes as "the antique store that time forgot because it's never open."

He actually does open the place on rare occasions, but mainly it serves as overflow storage for his antiques. In the basement is a vault-like room that houses part of his collection of old guitars and a smattering of fiddles, lap-steel guitars and a viola or two, and another room stuffed with more antiques. Among the curious items in his collection is Johnny Cash's Alcoholics Anonymous book, signed by former first lady Betty Ford, and A.P. Carter's zither.

A.P. Carter was the patriarch of the Carter Family, one of the most famous and influential acts in early country music, and a zither is an instrument similar to an autoharp. Having A.P. Carter's zither is like owning Babe Ruth's favorite bat.

Kostas still keeps a place in Nashville, but he spends most of his time in Belgrade, where he likes the idea of being able to walk just about everywhere he needs to go. He also likes Belgrade because in Nashville, too many people are "pursuing the bottom line, which is the dollar, instead of the top line, which is loving what you do."

He writes most of his songs early in the morning, getting up at 3 or 4 and working for a few hours. He says he gets into a dreamlike state when he's writing, usually working out a melody first.

"Pretty soon a pattern develops and the words start to form," one line leading to the next. He works from reality, tapping into his own experiences. One song, "That's My Ocean," developed because Kostas used to write songs on the porch of his house in Nashville.

The trees were so dense in the neighborhood that he could hardly see anything else as he sat there day after day, thinking and musing. One day he realized he wasn't seeing the trees anymore. He was looking through them at a world of his own imagining.

Another song was born. He wrote about how he'd "stare across the street at my neighbor's yard and trees/ and dream till it's time for me to sleep."

And then the chorus:

" 'Cuz that's my ocean/ this chair's my island/ this beer's my mai-tai/ and that cooler's my palm tree/ honey pass me some lotion/ don't step on my castle in the sand/ I know that you don't understand, but that's my ocean."

Kostas wrote "That's My Ocean" four years ago and hasn't sold it yet, which isn't unusual. He figures he's written 1,500 songs since 1989, and maybe 200 of them have been recorded. It's getting harder to sell to Nashville these days, he says, because his songs haven't changed much, but the industry has.

He still writes songs about real things like heartache and disappointment and love and loss, all those things that country music used to tap into so well. But most of today's Nashville stars only want to sing songs that make them look good, Kostas says. They don't want to be the lonely or lovelorn guy.

He figures the industry might come around again and realize that real people want to listen to real songs.

After all his decades in the business, after all those songs and all the ups and downs, Kostas can wait.

Originally published August 4, 2006, in The Billings Gazette

SUGAR'S STINK

BILLINGS — Standing next to the big cylinders on the second floor of the diffuser plant at the Western Sugar Cooperative's Billings factory, where hot water runs over shredded beets 24 hours a day 4½ months a year, you're at Stink Central.

This is the point of origin for the smell that most pungently characterizes autumn in the Magic City.

Not that Brad Zitterkopf, the factory production manager in charge of the laboratory, is willing to admit it.

"What odor?" he says. "You keep talking about an odor. I don't know what you're talking about."

He's only joking, but he's serious when he says factory workers, even those who toil in the dense, foglike steam created by the sugar-diffusion process, get used to the odor quickly and barely notice it after a few days.

For the rest of us, the sharp, acrid, slightly sweet scent of sugar beets is part of our lives during what is known as the annual beet campaign, which generally runs from the end of September to about Valentine's Day.

Zitterkopf says there's nothing too arcane about the process that produces the odor. "It's just the proteins or vegetable matter of the beets denaturing or cooking." The odor is similar to what you'd smell if you cooked a beet on your kitchen stove.

"We're just doing it on a very large scale," he says.

Make that very, very large. In an average year, the Billings factory, the oldest part of which was built in 1906, will process nearly 1.4 billion pounds of sugar beets, or about 400 million individual beets. They will be refined into the equivalent of 4 billion restaurant-size packets of sugar.

To manufacture that much sweet, you have to create a lot of stink.

The beets are trucked into Billings from 26,000 acres of farmland in the region. After a three-stage washing process that removes rocks, weeds and dirt, the beets travel by conveyor belt to the diffuser plant, where they are shredded into long, narrow slivers called cossettes. The cossettes, which resemble small french fries, are then fed into the diffusers, two 60-foot-long cylinders with big steel corkscrews inside them.

These corkscrews, perforated to allow the passage of water, move the cossettes up the sloped diffusers. While the cossettes zip through the diffusers at the rate of 200 tons an hour, water heated to 140 degrees Fahrenheit washes over them, extracting their sucrose. Steam is also introduced into the diffusers, raising the air temperature as high as 165 degrees.

The sugar water that leaves the lower end of the diffuser is known as "raw juice," which goes through several more purifying and filtering steps before being sent to evaporators to remove excess water. The juice is then crystallized and separated into pure sugar and molasses. The molasses is mixed with the leftover beet pulp to be sold as livestock feed. The sugar goes into your coffee.

That's a simplified explanation of a process involving a sprawling factory that employs 250 people during the 4½-month campaign, but as far as the stink goes, the diffusion process is really all you need to know about.

Factory manager Ken Bennett says the odor doesn't emanate from any of the dryer stacks, the coal-fired boiler stack or any of the many vents scattered around the factory. The odor simply rises up out of the cooking process in the diffusers and seeps out of the factory and into the air.

Zitterkopf says the process is constant, so that generally the odor doesn't change. In an especially wet year, when the beets come out of the ground coated with mud, they might start going bad earlier than usual, creating a more pungent smell, but that happens rarely. This year, if anything, the ground was too dry, which sometimes causes the tapered "tails" of the beets to snap off as they're being pulled from the earth.

If the beet smell seems stronger on a given day, it's most likely because of the wind direction or atmospheric conditions. An inversion, for instance, might trap air in the valley and intensify the odor.

Although some people find the odor disagreeable or even disgusting, others hardly notice it, while still others find it almost pleasing.

Mayor Chuck Tooley, who has spent 30 of his 56 years in Billings, said he's more or less neutral on the scent, which he attempted to describe as "something humid," or something produced by a "hot, humid process," which is correct, if not terribly evocative.

Tooley has been the mayor of Billings for eight years, and in all that time, he said, only one person has ever raised the issue of the sugar beet smell with him. That was his wife, Joanie, who moved here in 1998.

"And you know what?" Tooley said. "Joanie says she likes it."

Originally published October 15, 2003, in The Billings Gazette

JOHNNIE LOCKETT THOMAS:
THE MEMORY KEEPER

I first wrote about Johnnie Lockett Thomas in 2002 when, in the wake of the 9/11 attacks, she found herself on a "master terrorist" list that made her life hell every time she tried flying anywhere. Somehow, the government had confused Johnnie, a 70-year-old black grandmother from Miles City, with a 27-year-old white man from Oregon who was wanted for murder and who happened to be using the alias John Thomas Christopher.

I went to Miles City to interview her for a column about her travails as a master terrorist and somehow — she loved to talk and you never knew where her stories would end up — the conversation got around to Horace Bivins, a buffalo soldier whose story I tell on Page 121. When I came to write about Bivins a year after that encounter with Johnnie, she provided some key facts for me and pointed me toward some useful source materials.

In the course of our conversations, I also learned that Johnnie was working on a book about her late husband, a native of Miles City named Bill Thomas, and I decided to write about that, too. To be honest, I think I would have found another excuse to write about Johnnie even if she hadn't been working on the book. She was one of the best conversationalists I ever met, vivacious, curious, brimming with wit, given to punctuating her stories and anecdotes with bursts of rolling laughter and theatrical hand gestures. Nine months after I wrote about Johnnie's book project, I wrote about her one more time, updating readers on her fight against inoperable cancer. She was as spunky and inspiring as ever, though her once boundless energy was clearly ebbing. She died less than a month later, at the age of 75.

MILES CITY — Growing up in Tuskegee, Ala., Johnnie Lockett knew almost nothing of far-off Montana, and she certainly hadn't heard of Miles City.

In 1953, the year Johnnie graduated from college, her friends set her up on a blind date with a young soldier who was attending Officer Candidate School at nearby Fort Benning, Ga. It wasn't very reassuring to hear him described as short, fat and silent, but Johnnie decided to give it a try.

The blind date was an outing with a group of Johnnie's friends, and the soldier, Bill "Bunky" Thomas, was soon asked where he was from.

Johnnie recalled, "He said, 'Miles City, Montana.' Well, there's a conversation stopper." As the evening wore on, it developed that Thomas didn't dance or play cards. And when Johnnie sat down at a piano to lead a singalong, Thomas said he didn't sing, either.

Late in the evening, however, when they finally had a few minutes alone, Thomas opened up and started talking, and Johnnie realized she had met someone whose outlook on life almost exactly matched her own. They were both Episcopalians, for one thing, which was unusual enough, but Johnnie said they also had the same way of looking at life and questions of morality.

She made the additional discovery that while Thomas might be reserved in company, here was a man who could spin a yarn. He talked about growing up in the wild Western town of Miles City. He talked about his great-grandfather Vernon Thomas, a Scotch-Irish cavalryman who married Sadie Butler, an African-American maid for Gen. Nelson A. Miles, the first commander of Fort Keogh, at the junction of the Tongue and Yellowstone rivers, in 1876. He talked about his other great-grandmother, Susie Hunter, who was the daughter of Moses Hunter, an ex-slave and buffalo soldier, the name the American Indians gave to black troops. And he talked about the people he knew growing up in Miles City, people like "Buckskin" Ethel, "Three-Finger" Red and "Big Nose" George Parrott.

Thomas talked, and Johnnie fell in love.

"I married my husband because of the wonderful stories he told me," she said.

Now, a year after she was diagnosed with inoperable cancer, Johnnie Lockett Thomas, 74, is racing to finish a project she has been working on for more than 30 years: writing an account of her late husband's early life. It is written in the first person, told from her husband's perspective, and she plans to call it "Growing Up Black in Montana."

Johnnie and Bill Thomas were married in 1954. Johnnie's father had always insisted that she sign a contract with the man she was going to marry, and one stipulation of the contract she and Bill worked out was that he would get a college degree. She had already earned a degree in drama and speech from Drake University in Iowa, but Bill had only graduated from Custer County High School, in 1948.

Tuskegee was an oasis of black culture during Johnnie's childhood. It was home to Tuskegee Institute, later Tuskegee University, where black professors taught black students, and to the third-largest Veterans Administration hospital in the country. It, too, was run by and for African-Americans, including Johnnie's father, who was badly wounded and gassed in World War I.

"Nobody in our home ever talked about whether we were going to college. It was just a given," Johnnie said.

Her husband duly continued his education and eventually earned a master's degree in public administration. He had a long career as an executive with the U.S. Postal Service. For years, he worked for James V. Jellison, who was a native of Forsyth and an assistant to the postmaster general.

During Bill's earlier career in the Army, he and Johnnie lived in Austria, Italy and Germany. With the Postal Service, they lived in Los Angeles; Bakersfield, Calif.; Washington, D.C.; and New Jersey. Bill also had temporary assignments that took him to San Francisco, Texas, Connecticut, China, and Trinidad and Tobago.

Soon after they met, Johnnie, endlessly fascinated by Bill's stories, began doing research about Miles City, and about Montana and the West. She was surprised to find that even some of his more fanciful yarns and far-fetched claims were borne out by the discoveries she was making in archives and libraries. Johnnie always loved to research and write, but mostly in an academic vein. In the mid-1970s, she started stitching together her husband's Miles City stories, putting his history into the form of a first-person narrative. That was another thing she learned from her husband.

"He kept telling these stories, and he said that's all history is, is a series of stories," Johnnie said.

Johnnie has about 135 clean pages written, with countless more in rougher, unedited shape. Many of her finished chapters tell of the characters in her husband's family and in early-day Miles City. One of the first things Johnnie had to do was to untangle Bill's "very convoluted" family history. There are gaps and question marks, but the main characters in the book include a great-great-grandfather, Moses Hunter, and his daughter Susie. Other important figures were great-grandparents Vernon and Sadie Thomas.

Sadie, Gen. Miles' maid, came from Philadelphia by way of Fort Leavenworth, where she worked as a cook. She arrived in Montana with Miles in 1876, the year he was sent out to establish Fort Keogh. When relay stations for tending horses and wagons were needed along the Yellowstone River, Sadie was sent out to run the first one, about 15 miles west of Fort Keogh.

The spot was known as Sadie for many years, and a nearby stream was named Sadie Creek. Sadie's husband, Vernon Thomas the cavalryman, arrived in Miles City a year after Gen. Miles. He was supposed to rendezvous with Miles, who was in the field when Thomas arrived, so Thomas rode out to meet him. Johnnie said he spent his first night at the relay station.

"That's how I am told that he met her," she said. However it was, by sometime in 1878 it was general knowledge that the two were in love. It wasn't easy being a white man in love with a black woman in those days. Johnnie tells the story of how a man called Vernon Thomas a "nigger lover" in a Miles City saloon.

The two got in a brawl, and the man shot Thomas. Thomas survived, and when his Army comrades threatened to lynch his assailant, the man was released from custody and allowed to make his escape to Texas. And when Vernon Thomas' mother came to visit from Philadelphia in 1897, Johnnie writes, "the whole community joined in the conspiracy of passing off Sadie as Vern's cook and his children as Mexican workers."

Bill Thomas was raised by his great-grandmother Susie and his great-great-grandfather Moses. Johnnie said her husband was born illegitimate, and Susie heard rumors that a baby in the hospital might be the offspring of her grandson, a man named George. So she marched down to the hospital, identified which baby was George's — to her own satisfaction, at least — and took him home to raise him. Nobody tried to stop her because she was a strong-willed, "absolutely outrageous" woman, Johnnie said.

Susie sold whiskey to the Cheyenne Indians who lived near Miles City but were officially prohibited from buying alcohol. Johnnie writes: " 'They got as much right to get drunk as anybody else,' Grandma believed, especially when there was profit to be made from it. She ran a thriving bootlegging business."

Moses didn't die until 1942, and the former slave who also fought for the Union in the Civil War became the oldest veteran of that conflict in Miles City. He used to give speeches on Armistice Day, Johnnie said. One time Bill Thomas came home from school and said he had learned that Abraham Lincoln freed the slaves. Johnnie said Moses pounded the table with his fist and told the young boy, "Nobody freed me, sir, nobody. I freed myself with a pitchfork and a gun. Don't you forget it, sir; don't you ever forget it." Then he unbuttoned his shirt to show his great-great-grandson the scars on his chest. He had been whipped as a slave.

Much of the book tells of Bill Thomas' own days in Miles City, growing up at a time when, according to Johnnie, you could probably have counted all the African-Americans in town on the fingers of one hand.

"Being black here in Miles City was much harder than people would like to think," Johnnie said. Bill gradually earned the respect of most kids his age, Johnnie said, but only after "beating the hell" out of every other boy in school. He also worked hard at multiple jobs, since he was the main support of his family, and Johnnie said he was the first "recognizable" black student — there may have been others who "passed" for white — to graduate from Custer County High. He also played football in high school.

Bill worked for the railroad during and just after high school, but when he was told he could never join the union because he was black, he enlisted in the Army, leaving Miles City in 1951. Johnnie and her three children often visited Miles City over the years, but they never lived there as a family. When Bill died in 1995, Johnnie and her children took him back to Miles City to be buried. They were amazed at the reception they received. Although Bill hadn't lived there since he was a young man, the church was packed for his funeral service. People started telling Johnnie new stories about her husband, and she learned that many people considered him a hero.

There was even talk of inducting him into the Range Rider Museum Hall of Fame. A year later the induction took place, and Johnnie went back to Miles City to witness the honor, the first time it had been bestowed on an African-American.

"It was the most moving event of my life," she said. "It was just stunning."

She was still living in New Jersey at the time and had been looking around the country for a new place to settle down. After the museum induction, she was heading to the airport to fly home when she noticed an apartment with a "for rent" sign. When she got home she called the Postal Service, which had offered to help her move, and asked to have her belongings shipped to Miles City. Her friends, she said, thought she was "totally insane," but Johnnie calls it the best decision she ever made.

She threw herself into her new life, doing more researching and writing and getting involved in the community. She encountered racism, just as her husband had decades earlier, but by and large she loved her life in the West. When her cancer was diagnosed in 1999, she was overwhelmed by the willingness of people to help her. People brought her food, ran errands for her, gave her rides and offered her comfort.

"It was the whole town," Johnnie said. "I'm talking about a town where even people who hated me, when I got sick, they helped me."

In the first week of March 2006, on the fifth anniversary of being cancer-free, Johnnie was diagnosed with inoperable cancer. After a spell in the hospital, she demanded to be sent home. She was, with morphine and home health aides. She continued getting chemotherapy treatments until December, when she was so weak she could barely function.

She decided she had to quit chemo if she wanted to get anything done, including writing the story of her husband's life. "So far," she said, four months later, "I'm feeling absolutely great."

She knows she's on borrowed time, but she's determined to make the best of what's left.

"I want this book done desperately," she said. "My husband wanted it finished so badly."

Originally published March 31, 2007, in The Billings Gazette

MAKING MUSIC ON THE PRAIRIE

The Prairie Winds Café in Molt, Mont., seats 56, which is about four times the population of Molt itself. Yet on most Saturday mornings, every seat is taken, and another 15 or 20 people are standing in the hallway near the kitchen, patiently awaiting their turns.

It's not just Fran Urfer's pies that bring people in. Nor is it simply the setting — a tiny island of commerce in a sea of rolling grassland that runs to the foot of the Crazy Mountains in south-central Montana. What draws folks from miles around — and from every state in the nation and 42 foreign countries, according to the guest book — is the live music played there on Saturday mornings from 9 to noon.

Jerry and Fran Urfer opened the café in 2001, after spending three years remodeling Kepferle Mercantile, an old general store that featured hardware on one wall and groceries on the other. The music was Larry Larson's idea. He lived just down the road and thought the café would be a fine place for his band, The Hogback Five, to get in some practice.

"The first thing you know, we had some other bands coming out," Larson says. "Now, if you want to play here, it won't be in

2010. They might squeeze you in in 2011."

Customers have to squeeze in, too, often sharing a table with strangers and then parting as friends before the morning is over.

They call it the Bluegrass Saturday Breakfast, but the 10 or 12 local bands in the Prairie Winds' rotation also play old-time country, folk, and gospel. You might even hear a little Cajun, Dixieland, or vintage rock 'n' roll.

"It's been the funnest thing in my life," says Dave Webinger, a 69-year-old barber and guitarist whose band, Cold Frosty Morning, was playing in Molt the Saturday before Christmas. "We all work, so we just play for fun."

The bands also play for tips, their fiddle and mandolin cases slowly filling with greenbacks, and Fran treats them to breakfast and lunch.

Molt is 20 miles from Billings, the biggest city in Montana, but out on the empty prairie, it might as well be frontier days. The café, on Wolfskill Avenue, still features the building's original pressed-tin ceiling and fir flooring.

Molt was a thriving grain-hauling hub until the railroad pulled out 30 years ago. Now the town consists of five houses, a church, a tiny school, a tire shop, a grain elevator, a fire department, and a community hall. The Prairie Winds put Molt back on the map.

The place is aptly named, too. It's a rare day when the flag at the post office next door isn't snapping smartly in a stiff breeze. It's almost as rare not to find at least one dog snoozing in the shelter of the café's entryway.

"This, to me, is America," says the Rev. Bill Vibe, the Los Angeles-based interim pastor of the Congregational church in nearby Laurel. Vibe had come to the kitchen just before noon to compliment Fran on her cooking and tell her how much he liked the café. "We've sat here since 9:30 this morning, and I just had the time of my life," he says.

Fran says people thought she and Jerry were crazy when they talked about opening a café in Molt, but now it's not unusual to go through 20 dozen eggs on a Saturday morning, and every week she hears from people like Bill Vibe. "That's what makes it worthwhile," she says, "when people come in the kitchen and say things like that."

ROY YOUNG:
LIVE AT THE CRYSTAL LOUNGE

BILLINGS — It's 9:15 p.m. at the Crystal Lounge, the Saturday before Christmas, and Roy Young is swinging into "Just Walk on By," his first song of the night.

Before he finishes the guitar introduction, the back door flies open and Santa Claus strides in, accompanied by another man dressed as one of his elves. It's still early, but Santa already looks as though he might need a designated driver.

Roy doesn't miss a beat. As he adjusts the controls on his drum machine with his right hand, he leans into his microphone and shouts out, "Hello, Santa!" Then, as Santa and his elf circulate through the lounge distributing hugs and candy canes, Roy whips out a guitar medley of Christmas songs, jazzing them up or throwing in country licks as the spirit moves him.

He ends the medley with a blaze of picking, bends down to the microphone and says, "Once again, ladies and gentlemen, I'd like to welcome you to the Crystal Lounge."

Once again indeed. Roy has been at the Crystal Lounge in downtown Billings for 11 years, working as a guitarist and singer, a one-man band and the life of his own party. Roy's world revolves around the little bandstand tucked into the southeast corner of the Crystal, a long, narrow bar where red lights illuminate red furnishings and red flocked wallpaper.

Roy's got a drum machine and a set of foot pedals on which he plays a bass line, but basically it's just Roy and his guitar, a battered, beautiful Fender Telecaster, which he bought new in 1954. Roy knows rock songs and swing and pop and jazz, but most of his repertoire is classic country — hundreds of songs by the likes of Marty Robbins, George Jones, Hank Snow, Merle Haggard, Lefty Frizzell, Hank Williams and Willie Nelson.

If somebody shouts out a request, or steps up to the bandstand to sing a song with Roy, his right hand starts picking and his left hand starts running up and down the neck, as if the memory of each song were stored in his fingers.

Roy started out working a few times a week at the Crystal, but for the past six years he's been playing five nights a week, Tuesday through Saturday, every week of the year. In all that time, Roy has never taken a vacation, never called in sick.

In August, after marrying his second wife, Marie, Roy did take Wednesday off so they could have a three-day honeymoon. They had reservations at Fairmont Hot Springs, between Butte and Anaconda, but at the last minute Roy got a hankering to visit Jackpot, Nev. They drove down, spent a day and a half in Jackpot and drove back. Thursday night, Roy was back on stage.

By 9:30 the Crystal is slowly filling up. Roy can hardly get through a song without hailing some friend or other, announcing a birthday or promoting the Crystal's Sunday-night jam session.

Santa's out on the dance floor by now, and Roy interrupts a song to say, "Hey, Santa, you're lookin' pretty damn good out there." He's about to sing again when the back door opens. Roy spots a friend and a smile lights up his face. "How you doin', brother?" he says, then looks out and sees another friend: "Hello, brother Larry!"

Just before launching into "House of Blue Lights," a boogie-woogie number, Roy points to a woman sitting near the bandstand. "Michelle, honey," he says, "stand up — if you can." He looks out at the crowd and adds, "She's been drinkin' all night."

And Roy doesn't forget the help. "We've got some lovely cocktail waitresses," he says. "You all make sure you take care of 'em because they're workin' hard. Ain't that the truth."

Between the singing and the constant patter, Roy's voice is sounding a little strained this evening. But no matter. People come to the Crystal to listen but also to sing. At 9:45, Jim Jenkins, a big man wearing a brown cowboy hat, strolls up to the bandstand, consults briefly with Roy, grabs a spare microphone and belts out "Muleskinner Blues." It's obvious they've done this before. At the end of each chorus, Roy plays a bass line that perfectly matches Jim's slightly cracked yodeling.

Jim and Roy are singing "Storms Never Last" when Santa and his elf make a noisy exit. Roy makes note of Santa's departure before flatpicking an introduction to "Tennessee Whiskey," on which Jim and his wife, Sharyl, sing a duet. As the song ends Roy lets out a whoop and tells his audience that what they just heard was "100 percent, homogenized, pure country music."

Roy was born in Oklahoma City in 1940, but his family moved the next year to Oakland, Calif. It was there, when Roy was 5 or 6 years old, that he fell in love with a guitar he saw in a pawn shop window. He begged his mother to buy it.

The family didn't have much money, Roy says, but his mother doted on him. She saved pennies for months until she had enough to buy the $14 guitar. Roy says that when she walked in with a jarful of pennies, "the guy at the pawn shop didn't even count 'em."

With the guitar in his hands, Roy found his calling.

"I couldn't really play it," he says with a laugh. "But it felt good. I liked the way it felt. I strummed that thing for hours and hours. I probably put a lot of gray hairs on my mother's head."

As he got older he started trying to duplicate what he was hearing on records, or he would turn on the radio and play along for half the day. When he was 12 or 13 he began hanging around other guitar players, picking up techniques and learning new songs.

"I don't know, it's an obsession," he says. "Just a burning desire to play the guitar."

Jim Jenkins' friend, Larry Benifiet, is in the Crystal this evening to celebrate his birthday. While Larry is singing "The Wreck of the Old 97," Jim talks about Roy.

"I play eight instruments, and I'll tell you what — Roy's the best guitar player in five states." And the Crystal is the place to be. "It's pretty much the hangout for all the local musicians," he says. "Country musicians."

Jack Vaughn, another Crystal regular with long roots in the music biz, joins Roy just before 11, singing "You Don't Have Very Far to Go."

The crowd is clapping for Jack when the song's over, but Jack puts a hand on Roy's shoulder and announces, "This here's Roy Young. I know most of you know Roy, but this is one of the best guitar pickers in the whole state of Montana."

The place is packed now and the dance floor is crowded. As usual at the Crystal, the crowd is impossible to pigeonhole. There are cowboys and Indians, bikers and aging hippies, old couples and young singles, yuppies, street people and everything in between.

At 11:15, Roy is joined by his 19-year-old son, Jason, an aspiring country singer whose voice suggests early Ray Price. He sings a handful of country classics, and at the end of each song his father heaps compliments on his head. Roy is having a blast, people are dancing and cheering and the barmaids are busy.

Except for a two-year hitch with the Army in Korea, music is all Roy has done. He started out playing clubs in California when he was 16 or 17, then traveled all over the country, mostly with three-piece country bands.

He moved to Billings in the late '80s so his then-wife could be close to her parents, who lived in Ashland. Roy did his first show as a one-man band after moving here, only because he couldn't find any musicians he wanted to play with at the time.

He was performing regularly at a couple of places, but when he drove past the Crystal Lounge, with its neon-lit curved facade at the corner of Broadway and First Avenue North, Roy made up his mind.

"I just wanted to play that club," he says. "It looked good."

He went in and talked to the bartender, Pete Nelson, who told him the Crystal had tried live music for a while but couldn't afford it. Roy said he'd play that night, for free. That was a Monday. He played Tuesday and Wednesday, too, and the crowd seemed to like it, and he was back the next week, still playing for free.

Larry Davidson, the owner of the Crystal, knew a good thing when he saw it. Roy was soon being paid, and eventually he expanded to four nights a week, Wednesday through Saturday. The full-time gig started after Larry broached the subject of bringing in a karaoke machine — they were all the rage then — on Sunday nights.

Larry says Roy "went ballistic," cursing karaoke machines as the enemy of all professional musicians. As an alternative, Roy proposed starting a Sunday-night jam session. It has evolved into a popular tradition, making Sunday nights at the Crystal as big as Fridays and Saturdays.

"I know a lot of musicians who can play, but Roy has a real rapport with the audience," Larry says. "He can play with anyone, and he can play anything."

At 11:45, Del Voegele is up singing with Roy. After a song or two, Del is joined by Jim Jenkins, and the two of them get into a yodeling contest. Roy keeps turning up the tempo on his drum machine, egged on by the crowd, until Del and Jim look ready to bust.

After the contest ends, Del throws back a drink and explains to the crowd that he's known Jim since they were little boys. He used to sit in Jim's basement, he says, with Jim trying to teach him how to yodel.

"That's why I'm stunted in growth," he says. "Every time I'd miss a yodel he'd hit me on the head."

After the yodeling contest, Del sings "Lucky Old Sun." He takes a bow afterward and turns to Roy. "Let's do 'Your Cheatin' Heart,' " he says. "I'll dedicate that to all my ex-wives."

As Del makes his way back to his table, Roy starts playing a guitar rag at breakneck speed, squeezing off frills, runs and chords but still looking as relaxed as he has all evening. At just past midnight, he finally takes his first break of the night.

Roy says he felt right at home at the Crystal from the first night he played there.

"The Crystal is more than a club," he says. "It's like a family of people. It's like playing in your front room."

He describes his bandstand as "about the size of a medium Jacuzzi." The worn carpet and all Roy's equipment are shrouded with dust and cigarette ashes, but when it's dark outside and the lights are low in the Crystal, nobody notices.

Roy owns at least 15 guitars, but his workhorse, the one that never leaves the club, is the '54 Telecaster. "If this guitar could talk," Roy says, "you know what it would say? It would probably say, 'Take me out and let me see the sunshine.'"

Roy likes the Telecaster because it's got a great feel, a good sound and few embellishments.

"That's like the Crystal Lounge," he says. "Not a lot of sophistication and complications."

The rest of his equipment is also fairly simple. Unlike a computer-based sound system, which has to be pre-programmed, Roy's rather primitive set-up allows him to improvise with the bass line, the tempo and the beat of each song.

In addition to the drum machine, which Roy adjusts by means of a control panel, he picks out bass notes with his left foot, playing what looks like the long wooden pedals on a church organ. With his right foot he plays another, rectangular pedal. This pedal changes the bass notes to minors, sevenths or minor-sevenths, depending on whether the pedal is depressed with the toe or heel, to the right or left.

As often as Roy plays the Crystal, you might think he wouldn't need to practice, but he does, every day. "I do a lot of exercises," he says. "You've got to keep your fingers nimble." He also adds four or five songs a week to his repertoire, mostly old country numbers, but new ones too, especially songs that are frequently requested.

No matter what he plays, Roy says, "all the tunes I do, I play 'em different every single night." He never has a set list, or any idea what he's going to play. He tries to pick up on the mood of the crowd before deciding what to play and how to play it.

"You work the emotions and the feelings of the people that are in the bar into the songs," he says. "I try to keep it very basic. You have to work it. If it wasn't for that, you might as well listen to a jukebox."

Roy's only break of the night is over by 12:25. Jack Vaughn is back singing again, this time with his wife, Bernie. They sing "Wine, Wine, Wine" together, and then Jack croons out "Somewhere, My Love." During the guitar solo, Roy does a pretty convincing job of making the Telecaster sound like a balalaika.

Roy gets the dance floor packed again while he plays "Maybellene," and at one point he manages to continue playing a lightning-fast rock 'n' roll lead with his left hand while waving goodbye to another friend with his right.

The bar is all in a whirl by 1:15 a.m. Dancers are pushing out from the dance floor into the first row of tables, friends of Roy are singing songs and the buzz of conversation, fueled by alcohol, is noticeably louder. While Buck Landregh is up at the bandstand singing "Blue Eyes Cryin' in the Rain," Del Voegele is shouting to be heard above the general din.

"Listen," he says, pointing at Roy. "He's the best there is in the whole United States." Del pauses for a moment and then gestures with his arms to take in the entire bar. "Listen. Don't give me no fanfare, but you're with the best people in the whole damn world."

Roy closes out the night with "La Bamba," sparking a sing-along on the catchy chorus. He's been on stage for slightly more than four hours, picking and singing and talking almost continually, playing something like 35 songs.

Roy signs off with another plug for the Sunday-night jam just as the bright lights come up at 1:40, signaling that it's time to finish your drink and hit the road.

Roy turns off his equipment, leans his guitar against an amplifier and threads his way past the bandstand railing to the dance floor. In the space of 20 feet he is alternately hugged, kissed and slapped on the back at least 15 times, leaving him rumpled and a little dazed as he sits down at the table where Marie, his wife, is patiently waiting.

Roy is asked if he's all done, and a big smile creases his face.

"We're never done," he says. "We're just gonna stop for a while."

Originally published December 30, 1999, in The Billings Gazette

FATHER PONESSA:
FROM BIGHORN TO THE BIBLICUM

GLENDIVE — Growing up in Bighorn, a flyspeck of a town at the junction of the Yellowstone and Bighorn rivers, the Rev. Joseph Ponessa lived next door to his grandmother, who spoke Italian.

He was very young, still learning to speak English, when he began asking her how to say words in her native tongue.

"I would say, 'How do you say window?' She would say, *finestra*. And I would say, 'Wow, who would have guessed it? *Finestra*.'"

It would be many years before he would become fluent in Italian, but Ponessa calls his grandmother "my first foreign language teacher." The sense of wonder he felt learning a language at her knee never left him.

In time, he would combine his love of language and his love of God to earn a doctorate in Scripture from the Pontifical Biblical Institute in Rome, something only 30 other Americans had done since the founding of the institute in 1909. Graduates of the Biblicum, as it is known, are required to learn at least nine languages, including Hebrew, Greek, Latin and Aramaic, the language spoken by Jesus.

Laurie Manhardt, a Catholic writer in Florida who has colla-borated with Ponessa on three books of Bible study, said she was amazed at his "breathtakingly beautiful" commentary on the Scriptures. She assumed most colleges and seminaries would love to have him on their faculties.

Even so, she said, "the most impressive thing about Father Ponessa is that he is a good, holy, faithful priest. He loves his vo-cation, he loves God's word and he loves his flock."

Ponessa has tended flocks in his native state since his ordina-tion 30 years ago, serving as a teacher and parish priest in each of the five vicariates, or administrative districts, of the Diocese of Eastern Montana. In that respect he is different from most of those who study at the Biblicum and who see it as a stepping stone to a career in teaching or scriptural research.

"I wasn't using the Biblicum as a way of getting out of being a diocesan priest," Ponessa said. "The knowledge of the word of God belongs in the church."

For all his scholarship, Ponessa wears his learning lightly. A short, balding, monkish-looking man, he speaks quietly, but with a clarity that makes all his remarks seem prepared — not re-hearsed or stuffy, but polished. He is so familiar with the Bible, and he knows so much about the ancient world in general, that facts, anecdotes and history lessons spill out of him naturally, without a whiff of pedantry.

At a Bible study class for high school students at his Sacred Heart Church in Glendive one December night, Ponessa led a discussion about various biblical passages dealing with horses. Before long he was talking about the role of horses in the wars of the ancient Middle East and of Rome.

He told his students about the temple of war in Rome, which was large and frequently visited, and of the much smaller and neglected temple of peace. Rome, he said, was the only su-perpower at one time, and it had to fight on many borders. He found occasion to mention the Tigris and Euphrates rivers, ask-ing the young students if those names rang any bells, and soon he was talking about current events in Russia, Turkey and Ukraine.

At intervals, the background chatter threatened to drown out the Bible discussion, and Ponessa could hardly be heard above the din. If the students knew anything of his intellectual attainments, they didn't appear daunted by them. Ponessa, for his part, seemed not only patient but almost unaware of the jokes and rowdy asides swirling around him, pressing on in his calm voice.

The next morning, the 56-year-old Ponessa led an adult Bible study class for about a dozen people, all of them considerably older than he. His style and manner of speaking didn't change. He was still the quiet, patient teacher and fellow searcher.

In that class, he spoke of the evil of abortion, which he talked about in the context of the killing of other innocents, from genocide and the use of nuclear weapons to the deaths of civilians in modern warfare.

From there, he was soon deep into a description of Germany under Hitler, Italy under Mussolini and Spain under Franco. Self-expression is the first thing that disappears under totalitarianism, Ponessa said, and he got the elderly students laughing by asking them to imagine an Italy where the citizens are afraid to speak in public.

At the conclusion of the class, which began and ended with an examination of the New Testament letters of John, Ponessa delivered a few final remarks, then shrugged and said with a smile, "That's my opinion, anyway."

As small and isolated as Bighorn might seem to some, Ponessa said it was "an amazing little immigrant community," a "little U.N.," when he was growing up there in the early 1950s. There were Belgians and Italians and Yugoslavians, and lots of people from the American South. His mother, Mary Feeley, was Irish, and his father, also Joseph Ponessa, was Italian. Both were devout Catholics, and like most everyone else in the area, they were farmers.

Ponessa attended school through the fifth grade in Bighorn and sixth through eighth in Custer, on the other side of the Bighorn River. He said he decided in the third or fourth grade that he wanted to be a priest.

"I suppose the fact that I had asthma and couldn't farm had something to do with it," he said. There was also some family precedent for his decision: his grandfather's first cousin was a monsignor in New York, and his grandmother's sister was a nun.

Asked if his later love of Rome, and particularly the antiquities of Rome, might have had its origins in his being raised in an area where written history was so recent and monuments so few,

Ponessa said no.

"I thought the hills of Eastern Montana were monumental. I feel I've grown up surrounded by monuments."

After elementary school, Ponessa enrolled at Assumption Abbey, a Catholic prep school in Richardton, N.D. He had four years of "pretty serious" Latin there, in the course of which he recalled making another linguistic discovery.

"I remember the shock of finding out that *bello* meant 'beautiful' in Italian and 'war' in Latin. Something went terribly wrong somewhere."

From Assumption Abbey he went to Mount Angel Seminary in St. Benedict, Ore. Why? Because he was a good Catholic. "The bishop said, 'Go there,' so I went."

At seminary, students spent four years earning the equivalent of a bachelor's degree and four years earning a master's in theology. For his first degree he studied literature and wrote his thesis on the works of German novelist Hermann Hesse.

He studied theology under Abbot Bonaventure Zerr, whom Ponessa credits with being one of his great inspirations. Zerr inspired him by believing in him, by encouraging him to take on difficult tasks, whether it was the study of Arabic or his decision to seek a doctorate from the Biblicum.

Actually, that was a decision Ponessa had made in high school, after hearing of a priest who had gone partway through the process of earning a doctorate there. His reason for setting such a goal seems disarmingly simple.

"It sounded like a challenge," he said. "I always thought, give me a hoop and I'll jump through it. Give me a hoop, any hoop."

Most students pursue a doctorate at the Biblicum as you would a conventional degree, by attending school continuously until graduation. Ponessa, because he wanted to be a parish priest, didn't allow himself that luxury. Instead, for nearly 15 years, he prepared himself for his studies in Rome by taking college-level language courses through summer school programs.

Then, at the age of 37, he started his studies at the Biblicum, spending another 15 years working toward his doctorate. He managed to put in two continuous years in Rome over the course of his studies, but to fulfill the rest of his requirements he would save up his vacation time each year and then spend three weeks or a month in Rome. He also used his own money to pay for his education.

As much as he loved Rome and the Biblicum, he said, "a person can only take so much. One vacation I ran away to Japan because it had absolutely nothing to do with the Bible."

During those 30 years of study, Ponessa was working all over Eastern Montana. His first posting after his ordination was in Billings, where from 1974 to '79 he was the priest at Holy Rosary Church and taught Latin and religion at Central High School.

There followed a year in Wolf Point, five years in Miles City, less than a year in Great Falls and seven years in Malta. For the past 11 years he has been in Glendive, where he is also the priest for St. Peter Church in Wibaux and St. Philip Church about 15 miles outside Wibaux.

Before enrolling at the Biblicum, Ponessa had studied Hebrew, Arabic, Greek, Latin, French, Italian and Spanish. In Rome, he began his study of Aramaic, the language in which several parts of the Old and New Testaments were written, and German, the last of the languages he needed for his degree.

German was hardest of all. After many years of intense study, he said, "I think I was just tired."

Biblicum students needed all those languages because they had to know the Scriptures in their original languages and also become familiar with the major languages in which Bible scholarship had been conducted over the centuries. Ponessa chose Arabic as one of his electives because it is closely related to Hebrew and thus useful for puzzling out the meaning of obscure biblical passages.

To be gone for such long stretches from his parish duties, Ponessa often found substitutes among his Third World colleagues at the Biblicum. Since they had little money to finance their educations, they welcomed the chance to work in the United States and earn enough to pay for another term in Rome.

Gene Fitzpatrick of Wibaux, a longtime friend of Ponessa's and a lay helper at Ponessa's parishes, said the result was that the Glendive and Wibaux churches have been served over the years by priests from India, Nigeria, Poland and Uruguay.

Fitzpatrick was one of three Montanans who accompanied

Ponessa to Rome on Jan. 12, 2001, where he had to defend his doctoral thesis before a panel of Jesuits. His thesis examined the Last Supper narratives in light of the "rhetoric of doubling," or the use of doubled elements, like two cups instead of one, in Luke and First Corinthians.

Fitzpatrick said he urged Ponessa to tell the Jesuits, most of whom were Irish, that he was part Irish himself, in hopes of softening their legendary severity. Ponessa ignored Fitzpatrick's advice.

"My Irish side was too stubborn to use it as an advantage," he said. "If they were not perceptive enough to notice my Irishness, I shouldn't have had to bring it up."

On the morning of his defense, Ponessa and another Montana friend, the Rev. Martin Fisher of Billings, were allowed to help Pope John Paul II celebrate a Mass in the pope's private chapel in the Vatican.

Ponessa practiced his Polish for a year before his audience with the pope and was able to say to him, in his native tongue, "God prosper you, Holy Father."

"I don't know what he said back," Ponessa admitted.

At a reception after Ponessa received his degree from the Biblicum, one of the Jesuit examiners took Fitzpatrick aside and told him to keep a watch on Ponessa when they returned to the United States. After years of arduous labor, capped by a huge accomplishment, he told him, there might be a letdown, even some depression.

Fitzpatrick felt there was no need to worry. It wasn't as if Ponessa had nothing else to occupy his mind.

Even while he was working toward his doctorate and attending to the myriad duties connected with his three parishes, Ponessa kept up with an astonishing range of other interests. He has played flute for 30 years, and he loves to listen to classical music and operas. He is also a big fan of the movies, of classic films domestic and foreign, science fiction, fantasy, musicals and comedy.

In the living room of his rectory in Glendive, which Ponessa calls his "escape room," he has some 800 laser discs of movies and classical music performances, which he watches on a TV with a 55-inch screen. Down the hall is his library, with hundreds of works in the many languages he knows.

"That's the purpose of travel, isn't it?" he said. "To spend everything you've got on things to lug home?"

He is also a photographer who has compiled, again on laser disc, pictures of virtually every ancient building and monument in Rome. Years ago, he sold copies of the disc — accompanied by a bound volume telling the story behind each building and monument — to help finance his studies. He is working on another project of photographing monasteries in Europe and the United States and matching them with Gregorian chants.

And in addition to the language studies connected with his degree, Ponessa has delved into others on his own. He has studied Akkadian, an extinct Semitic language, Polish and, most recently, Nahuatl, the language of the Aztecs. He is studying Nahuatl mainly because that is the language used to record the visions of Juan Diego, to whom the Virgin Mary is said to have appeared in 1531, triggering the conversion of millions of native Mexicans to Christianity.

What sets Ponessa apart from most intellectuals, according to a good friend of his, is that he does not restrict his interests to high-brow subjects.

Elizabeth McNamer of Billings, a Bible scholar who has known Ponessa since his ordination, said nothing is trivial to Ponessa, who believes everything is worthy of study and consideration.

"He's got a mind that just wants to take everything in. I mean everything," she said. Some years ago, Ponessa told McNamer that he really didn't understand football and wanted to learn more about it.

"The next time I saw him," she said, "he knew absolutely everything there was to know about football."

And while there are many zealous fans of the first "Star Wars" movie, Ponessa fed his fanaticism in his own unique way. After seeing the movie more than 40 times, he translated all his favorite lines into Latin.

"It was into very good classical Latin," he explained. "Not late Church Latin, but Latin as Caesar would have spoken it."

Some people wonder why Ponessa has remained a Montana parish priest all these years, but his friends seem to understand his decision very well.

Manhardt, who described her role as Ponessa's co-author as one of taking his "brilliance and making it lay-person friendly," said he is "a treasure of the church" whom one would expect to see in a much higher position.

"Yet, hearing confessions, saying Mass, preparing couples for marriage, visiting the sick and the prisoners may be more pleasing in the eyes of God than teaching in a college," she said. Manhardt said Ponessa "shows each of us how to be content, doing whatever work God gives us to do in whatever station of life God calls us."

McNamer agrees that Ponessa ought to be teaching at a college, but she sees another possible reason for his staying in Montana. Being in Glendive, she said, "gives him time to do all the things that he wants to do."

For Ponessa, whose parents still live in Custer, the explanation is even simpler.

"I'm a Montanan," he said. "I was never tempted to leave."

Originally published December 19, 2004, in The Billings Gazette

BEN STEELE:
FROM HORROR TO HEALING

BILLINGS — In 1994, almost 130 years after the end of the Civil War, an incredible collection of watercolor paintings depicting the experiences of one Union soldier was discovered.

"Eye of the Storm," a book based on the paintings and diaries of Pvt. Robert Knox Sneden, was finally published in 2000. Among his wide-ranging experiences in the Civil War, Sneden spent time in the infamous Confederate prison camp in Andersonville, Ga.

At its height, 30,000 soldiers were crammed into the 26-acre camp, making it the equivalent of the fifth-largest city in the South. Food became nearly as scarce as medical help. In 14 months, 13,000 Union prisoners died at Andersonville.

Historians were already familiar with that sickening chapter of American history, but until Sneden's diaries and paintings were discovered, there had never been a fully illustrated description of life inside the prison. The publishers of Sneden's book were not exaggerating when they called his memoirs and paintings "a lasting achievement in human expression of the horrors of war."

We have our own Pvt. Sneden right here in Billings, and the same may be said of his paintings and drawings. In 93 starkly vivid works of art, Ben Steele chronicled his memories of the Bataan Death March and the 3½ years he spent in brutal Japanese prisoner of war camps.

Steele was a corporal in the Army Air Corps when he and 80,000 other American and Filipino soldiers were captured in the Philippines in the early stages of World War II. Thousands died on the 60-mile trek that became known as the Bataan Death March, and thousands more perished in POW camps.

Steele's Prisoner of War Art Collection, which is on permanent display at the Central Montana Historical Association museum in Lewistown, has been exhibited in Billings at various times over the years, and his works have illustrated books and magazine articles. The Gazette published a couple of stories about Steele last week, in conjunction with a reunion of Bataan survivors at the Holiday Inn, and I was lucky enough to finally meet him.

If you happened to overhear Steele talking about what he lived through between 1942 and 1945 but weren't quite close enough to make out exactly what he was saying and caught only the tone — quiet and matter-of-fact — you might have thought he was talking about a family vacation, or maybe his career as an art professor at what used to be called Eastern Montana College.

But he was talking about torture, starvation, misery and death. He was talking about having suffered from malaria, worms, heart problems, open sores, boils, lice, scabies, blood poisoning, maggots and beriberi. He was chronically underfed and overworked, and occasionally beaten.

At a prison in the Philippines, a Catholic chaplain administered last rites to him three times. As Steele recounted all of these horrors, he sometimes let loose, unexpectedly, with a hoarse chuckle or even a rattle of laughter.

This, I think, is what is meant by that overworked phrase "The Greatest Generation." The greatness of that generation, or at least of its exemplars like Steele, is that they are great without seeming so to themselves.

More amazing than what he endured was the man he became afterward. It is one thing to look at Pvt. Sneden's Civil War art. It is something else, a rare privilege, to look at Cpl. Steele's artwork at a time when we can still learn, firsthand, the deeper meaning of his experiences. Steele radiates a peacefulness that you can almost feel. It comes from having learned to count his blessings.

"I still never sit down to a meal that I don't appreciate," he said. Even the freedom of travel is a thrill. "If I want to go to Laurel," he says, half-laughing, "I go to Laurel, and nobody's going to stop me."

Steele's daughter, Rosemarie Steele, said art saved her father. "He got rid of all his anger and his bitterness. These pictures were his therapy."

Steele said he made a conscious decision to let go of his bitterness. It might sound trite coming from anyone else, but the weight of Steele's suffering gives him an unusual authority.

"Hatred's an awful, destructive force," he said. "You just hurt yourself. And I learned that. I finally decided I'd better get over it. And I did."

Originally published June 24, 2007, in The Billings Gazette

THE CORPS OF DISCREPANCY

The trip to Culbertson described in this story would never have taken place if David Grubbs and I had not already been going to Glendive to interview the Rev. Joseph Ponessa (see Page 103). We were told of several amazing artifacts and historical sites in Culbertson, but the way they were described was rather suspect. Still, I couldn't help being intrigued by the man who made the pitch, Pete Spaabeck. I had the sense that he was a character worth meeting, whether or not the story panned out. We decided to stop in Culbertson, a couple of hours north of Glendive, before pushing on to meet Father Ponessa.

As you'll see, the Culbertson trip was, technically, a bust. Nearly every marvel that Pete described to us was, well, not locatable. But I won't say we were the victims of a fraud. I think, rather, that Pete was over-enthusiastic, one of those people who desperately want to believe that there is more to the world than meets the eye. As one story after another evaporated under the heat of our investigation, I could see that Grubbs was running out of patience.

After going zero for three, he was feeling desperate. "If one more site turns out to be bogus," he said, "that's it. We're screwed. No story."

I laughed an indulgent laugh and said, on the contrary, that if we were finally shown one thing of actual historical interest, it wouldn't be much of a story at all. If, on the other hand, yet another claim didn't hold up to investi-

gation, we had a story, one that wouldn't resemble your average newspaper story, but one I couldn't wait to tell. I think I was right. Here it is.

CULBERTSON — I would love to be able to tell you that Gazette photographer David Grubbs and I were part of a team that made an important discovery about the Lewis and Clark Expedition.

I'd love to, but I can't.

Journeying almost into North Dakota on what we hoped would be a history-making excursion, we came back more or less empty-handed.

But think of it: Lewis and Clark themselves had been sent out to find an easy passage to the Pacific Ocean, and nobody considered their expedition a failure just because they encountered the Rocky Mountains. Like Lewis and Clark, we did our best, which was all we could do.

Our voyage of discovery was set in motion by Pete Spaabeck, who had called from Culbertson a few weeks earlier to say he knew of a spot on a sandstone bluff above the Missouri River where the great explorers had carved their signatures, or possibly their initials.

What made the claim at least remotely plausible was that Spaabeck also put me in touch with Robert Nay, a 67-year-old Culbertson native now living in Froid, who said that when his mother was a young girl she was taken by a neighbor lady, a Mrs. Jacobs, to look at the initials.

"She talked about that off and on her whole life," Nay told me. If Nay's mother were still alive she'd be nearly 100, which meant she would have seen the initials very early in the 20th century. She could never remember exactly where the initials were, and all Nay knew was that they were supposed to be somewhere between the bridge over the Missouri just south of Culbertson and the Diamond Ranch a little downstream.

There matters lay until a few years ago, when Nay told his friend Spaabeck about the purported inscriptions. Spaabeck and his buddy, Dennis Ueland of Antelope, both believed Nay, though few others did.

"We'd tell people and they'd laugh at us," Spaabeck said. "So we said, let's find it and they'll stop laughing at us."

Thus, two years ago this fall, Spaabeck and Ueland launched a canoe from the fishing access under the Culbertson bridge, went a couple of miles downstream and then headed upriver, as Lewis and Clark would have done in the spring of 1805. To Ueland and Spaabeck's way of thinking, the pyramid-shaped sandstone bluff just downstream of the bridge would have been the logical place for Lewis and Clark to get out and have a look-see, because it affords a commanding view of the country for miles around.

Sure enough, Spaabeck said. When they climbed up to the top, there the initials were. Maybe. In his zeal to prove Nay right, and to add to the luster of an area he clearly loves, it is possible that Spaabeck may have been inclined to exaggerate the legibility of what he found.

And now that I think back on it, I guess Spaabeck was a little vague when we talked on the phone. But Grubbs and I were going to Glendive for a couple of other stories anyway, and this Culbertson thing sounded like a good adventure at the very least.

Besides, Spaabeck sweetened the pot by describing — again, in rather indistinct terms — a buffalo jump and a cave full of Indian pictographs very close to Culbertson.

That's how I found myself climbing the bluff in question one afternoon in the fall of 2004 with Grubbs and Spaabeck, our disarmingly enthusiastic guide. When we got to the top, Spaabeck took us to the front of the formation, where two large, flat slabs of sandstone came to a sharp point. He stopped and stood facing one of the surfaces of rock, as if waiting for us to find the signatures ourselves.

All I could see were some initials, including G.B., J.F.K. and D.S. At last, Spaabeck spoke. "Quite an old rock, though, isn't it? I know that's where I'd go if I wanted to carve my initials."

Well, yes, we said, not wanting to be pushy, but where were the historically significant initials we had driven 400 miles to see? Spaabeck motioned toward a corner of the rock, saying he thought he remembered they were in that general area. We bent in for a closer look, carefully scanning the sandstone, until I thought I detected what looked like a faint, faded "W," a "W," moreover, very similar to the one William Clark inscribed on Pompeys Pillar.

THE BIG SKY, BY AND BY

If you squinted hard and looked at just the right angle, allowing shadows to fill in the indentations in the rock, it almost looked as though several other letters followed the "W." All in all, though, it didn't appear to be anything you'd want to notify the historical society about, and Grubbs said it couldn't possibly be photographed.

With nothing much else to do, we continued investigating other pieces of the bluff. At one point I found what looked like the deepest inscription of all, which read, "P.S. 9/1/02." I brought it to Spaabeck's attention and he studied it for a long moment.

"P.S.," he said. "Hey — Pete Spaabeck! That one's mine!" Now he remembered. He and Ueland had been up there on Sept. 1, 2002, and he had left his own engraving on the stone.

We were about ready to call it quits when Grubbs and I found another inscription, this one the most intriguing of all, consisting of these block letters: "LeWI." There was some slight, barely conceivable chance that Meriwether Lewis had left his imprint there, right?

Again, we had no way of knowing. But we took some pictures of the carving, with Spaabeck striking a pose in the background, and prepared to head back down.

Just before we started, Spaabeck turned and said, "Else comes to else, I imagine it'd make a story, wouldn't it?"

I supposed it would.

From there, accompanied by Nay, we drove upriver in the fading light of late afternoon to the confluence of Big Muddy Creek and the Missouri River, about five miles west of Culbertson. We had already seen a historical marker at the fishing access, which said that members of the Lewis and Clark Expedition had shot and wounded a number of grizzly bears earlier on their voyage, but finally managed to kill one at Otis Creek on April 28, 1805.

Spaabeck had told us that Otis Creek was now known as Big Muddy Creek, and the spot where the bear was killed was known as Grizzly Point. It was a beautiful spot, no denying it, particularly as the sun was going down in a blaze of orange and pink, and it was a moving experience to be right there, so close to where Lewis must have stood, firing at the bear.

I asked Spaabeck how long the spot had been called Grizzly Point. Just a few years, he said, and he ought to know, for he had named it himself. By then it was getting too dark for any further exploration, so we arranged to meet again the next morning.

After an early breakfast, we lit out south across the Missouri toward the buffalo jump Spaabeck had told us about. We pulled over to the side of a gravel road after having gone about 10 miles west and south of town. Spaabeck, accompanied by Nay, pointed up at a high cliff that dropped straight down to the road, just above the banks of the Missouri.

I could have sworn that when we had talked on the phone, Spaabeck said there was still a large heap of bones embedded in the riverbank, and that the site had been thoroughly researched by a team from the state of Montana.

I must have heard wrong. On this cold, windy morning, Spaabeck said he had only heard about the bones, which must be around there somewhere, and didn't the cliff look just like the perfect place for a buffalo jump? I asked if the site was officially known as a buffalo jump.

"There'll be more than one person'd tell you that was a buffalo jump there," he said, which he seemed to think had answered the question.

None of us was eager to scramble down the steep, snow-covered banks of the river to look for bones, so we piled back into our vehicles and headed for Kane's Grove, about 15 miles south of town.

Nay said his mother had been born near Kane's Grove, a narrow swale crowded with a tangle of aged ash trees huddled around a spring. Nay's Uncle Ivan reportedly had told him of some caves in the hills just above Kane's Grove where the walls were painted with American Indian pictographs.

Halfway there, we pulled over so Spaabeck could direct our attention back at a line of hills north of Culbertson. He pointed out the features — the forehead, bushy eyebrows, a chin, the neck, arms and torso — of a sleeping giant formation. The giant was easier to make out than the Lewis and Clark signatures, though I'm not sure I spotted the eyebrows.

"I think it's phenomenal," Spaabeck said. "Most people don't even know they've got a sleeping giant. They've got a lot of stuff around here they don't know about."

The sandstone formations above Kane's Grove did look promising. Carved by the elements into arches, turrets and vaulted chambers, the sandstone outcroppings looked like just the sort of places where caves would form, and where visitors would be inspired to leave pictographs.

It was only then, however, that we learned that neither Nay nor Spaabeck had actually investigated the caves, and they didn't know exactly where to find them. We commenced searching again, just as we had on the bluff above the river, but we found no trace of a cave, much less of any pictographs.

In a large hollow in the sandstone we did see some inscriptions, evidence that we had been preceded by explorers bearing the names of Jenny, Rachel, Chris and Ashley, among others.

By then it was time for us to be heading to Glendive, so we drove back to the road and prepared to take our leave. Spaabeck, however, wasn't quite through with us. Gesturing toward the east, he showed us what he said were known as the Three Buttes, a trio of hills overlooking the Missouri.

"I'll bet you 10 to one that Lewis was up there or sent somebody up to take a look around," he said.

Fearing that we were going to be asked to scour those hills for inscriptions, too, Grubbs and I started to get into our car. As we were doing so, Spaabeck hollered over, wishing to say one last thing.

"Next time," he said, as if sensing that perhaps we were less than perfectly satisfied with our various outings, "we'll show you the good stuff."

Originally published December 5, 2004, in The Billings Gazette

HORACE BIVINS:
MORE THAN A SOLDIER

I was standing in a cluttered junk shop in Missoula when I first became aware of Horace Bivins. I had pulled down an old book, "Fort Custer on the Big Horn, 1877-1898," and was surprised to learn of this amazing soldier, who had spent a portion of his life in Billings. Information on him was hard to come by, and it was years before I wrote about him.

A few years after the story appeared, I was contacted by a representative of the Oxford University Press, who told me of plans to publish something called the African American National Biography, edited by Henry Louis Gates Jr. The representative said she was calling me because I was an "expert" on Horace Bivins, who was being considered for inclusion in the biography. I didn't consider myself an expert, but since I was probably the first person to write about Bivins in at least 50 years, who else were they going to call?

The eight-volume African American National Biography was published in 2008 and includes my entry on Horace Bivins, much condensed from the article reprinted here.

One of the most decorated soldiers ever to call Billings home was born shortly after the Civil War on a farm in Virginia, the son of free black parents. Horace W. Bivins' military career was so varied and full of adventure that an early newspaper account wasn't exaggerating much when it said an account of his life "reads like fiction from the imagination of a pulp magazine writer."

Bivins (it rhymes with "givens"), who eventually reached the rank of captain, fought Apache Indians in Arizona and insurgent natives in the Philippines. Sent to Cuba during the Spanish-American War, Bivins and other soldiers in the all-black 10th Cavalry once came to the rescue of a hard-pressed Teddy Roosevelt and the Rough Riders. Years after retiring from the Army, Bivins volunteered for service again during World War I, when he was made a supply captain at Fort Dix, N.J. He was also said to have been the only man ever to win three Army marksmanship gold medals in one year, earning that distinction in 1894 while serving at Fort Keogh in Miles City.

William "Buffalo Bill" Cody tried to recruit the expert marksman for his traveling Wild West show, and The Billings Gazette reported in 1935 that, when Teddy Roosevelt made his final visit to Billings during World War I, "he made particular inquiries" about Capt. Bivins.

In addition to all those official exploits, Bivins was widely known in his adopted town for his gardening skills and for amassing a natural-history collection that included rare birds, lizards, snakes and artifacts from the Philippines.

It was a long way to such acclaim from his beginnings in Pungoteague, Accomack County, Va., on May 8, 1866. Some sources, even a book to which Bivins contributed several chapters, say he was born in 1862, but all later newspaper accounts, written from interviews with Bivins, say the year was 1866. It doesn't help much that the Accomack County census said Bivins was 5 years old in 1870, the eighth of nine children born to Severn and Elizabeth Bivins. That same census gives their last name as Bevans, one of several variant spellings of the family name.

His father was a farmer, but one who "spent much of his time in religious and educational work," according to "Under Fire With the Tenth U.S. Cavalry," the book Bivins co-authored. The census said of his mother only that she "keeps house." Young Bivins worked on the farm until he was 18, when he entered Hampton School as a work student and received his first military training.

"Having a very great desire for adventure and to see the wild West," as he put it in "Under Fire," he enlisted in the Army on Nov. 7, 1887.

After undergoing some training in Missouri, Bivins was assigned to Troop E of the 10th Cavalry, which he joined at Fort Grant, Arizona Territory, in June 1888. Over the next four years, he told The Gazette in 1935, "my troop took a prominent part in the campaigns against Geronimo, Apache Kid, and other Indian chieftains of the southwest."

It was during his four years in Arizona that Bivins took up shooting. The first time he ever shot a rifle, during target practice, he placed No. 2 in a troop of 60 men and was soon made a sharpshooter.

In April 1892, Bivins' regiment was ordered to Fort Custer in Montana. They passed through Billings on the way to Custer Junction and then had to march through a foot of fresh snow to Fort Custer on May 5. During the next six years in Montana, Bivins and his fellow "buffalo soldiers," as the Indians called the black troopers, also served at Fort Assiniboine near Havre. Newspaper accounts said their time in Montana was not particularly hazardous. Once they were called out to quell a strike on the Northern Pacific Railroad, and they had some minor troubles with Cree and Cheyenne Indians.

Bivins kept up his shooting record in Montana, representing his troop in 1892, '93 and '94 at departmental competition. In 1894 he carried off the first Army gold medal in carbine competition at Fort Sheridan, Ill., where he also won two other gold medals. In 1896, Buffalo Bill Cody reportedly offered Bivins a position in the Wild West show, shooting against Annie Oakley. Cody was said to have sought a furlough for Bivins and offered him $100 a month, but The Gazette reported that Bivins "was in line to become an ordnance officer and preferred the army routine to circus life."

When war with Spain was declared in April 1898, Bivins' regiment was ordered south. They left Fort Assiniboine on April 18, heading first to Wisconsin and then south by train.

"We received great ovations all along the line," as well as flags, cigars and "many other pleasantries," Bivins wrote in "Under Fire With the Tenth U.S. Cavalry."

As they moved farther south, the welcome grew considerably more muted. "The signs over the waiting room doors at the Southern depots were a revelation to us," Bivins wrote. "Some read thus: 'White waiting room.' On the door of a lunch room we read: 'Niggers are not allowed inside.' We were traveling in palace cars and the people were much surprised that we did not occupy the 'Jim Crow' cars, the curse of the South."

Before embarking for Cuba, they drilled at a camp in Tennessee. "And there were in our lines many Indian fighters who were anxious to get a whack at the Spaniards," Bivins said. They soon got their chance, arriving in Cuba in mid-June. They were involved in a lot of hard fighting and marching, often side by side with the First Volunteer Cavalry, known as the Rough Riders. At the battle of Las Guasimas, Bivins said, the Rough Riders were ambushed in a narrow valley, under attack from the front and rear. Elements of the 10th Cavalry, "adopting the method used in fighting Indians," advanced on the Spaniards through tall grass and so surprised them with a volley that the Spaniards rushed out of their ambush and abandoned their attack on the Rough Riders.

Bivins told a Billings Gazette reporter in the 1930s, "I don't think it an exaggeration to say that but for the timely aid of the Tenth Cavalry, the Rough Riders would have been annihilated."

Bivins' most notable service in Cuba, for which he was awarded a Silver Star, came during the famous battle of San Juan Hill. A sergeant by then, Bivins was assigned to a Hotchkiss gun battery. The Hotchkiss was a small artillery piece with a rifled barrel. With the other members of his detachment killed or wounded, Bivins single-handedly fired 72 shells from one of the Hotchkiss guns, which recoiled six to eight feet after each shot. His performance was all the more remarkable in that early in the battle he had been knocked out briefly by a slug that passed through an iron-plated hub of a gun carriage and hit him in the temple.

After some more service stateside and then a brief return to Cuba, Bivins' regiment was sent to the Philippines in April 1901 to "pacify" insurrectionist natives in the wild, swampy northeastern part of the main island. The regiment was busier clearing trails than in fighting natives, and after about a year they were shipped home and dispatched to Fort Missoula. Bivins made frequent trips to Billings, The Gazette later reported, because he was fond of the climate and of a certain Claudia Browning, whom he had met during his years at Fort Custer. Browning was a native of Deadwood, S.D., whose parents had come to Billings in 1883. Bivins married Claudia in March 1904, and they set up home at Fort Missoula, where they remained until he was ordered back to the Philippines in the summer of 1906.

Things were even quieter during his second stay there, so Bivins spent most of the next 19 months searching for and collecting Philippine birds, shells, fossils and other curios and artifacts. His collection eventually included two monkey-eating eagles, which he later donated to museums in Minneapolis and San Francisco.

"So excellent was the collection that Mr. Bivins brought back to America with him, that Mr. I.D. O'Donnell of this city purchased the greater part of it for the Parmly Billings Memorial Library," The Gazette reported in 1935.

Bivins returned to the United States for a four-month furlough late in 1907, and he returned to the Philippines early in 1908, expecting to stay there until he was eligible to retire. But War Department paper shufflers somehow got him transferred to the Presidio near San Francisco later that year, and Bivins ended up being transferred from fort to fort all over the country. He was an ordnance sergeant by then and was sent to various posts "to straighten up the affairs of that department." He finally retired from active service on July 13, 1913. With double-time credit for foreign service in Cuba and the Philippines, he was given credit for 30 years in the regular Army.

After his retirement, he settled in Billings, where he was known mainly for his flourishing gardens. Helen Adams, writing a sketch of Bivins that is preserved in the Parmly Billings Library Montana Room, said, "Things just grew for him. The most notable of his garden produce was the successful raising of sweet potatoes."

Horace and Claudia Bivins had two sons and a daughter and lived for many years on South 25th Street. Claudia was an active member of the African Methodist Episcopal Church, vice president of the Montana Federation of Negro Women, a member of the Society of Eastern Montana Pioneers and secretary of the

Billings Federation of Women's Clubs.

In 1918, after the United States had entered World War I, Bivins was recalled by the War Department and assigned to the ordnance department in Newport News, Va. In June of that year, the African republic of Liberia, founded in 1821 as a settlement for freed U.S. slaves, offered Bivins a commission to train 115,000 men who were going to fight against the Germans in West Africa. He declined and in September was made a captain of infantry, serving first as a supply officer at a detention camp at Fort Dix, N.J., then as head of a labor battalion in the same camp. He retired from the Army for good in 1919. He had by then 32 years of credit with the Army and, coincidentally, had won 32 Army medals.

He studied taxidermy after the war and followed that trade for many years. A 1935 article described him as "industrious, sober and studious." It also described him as being 6 feet tall, with broad, square-set shoulders.

In the book "On the Trail of the Buffalo Soldier: Biographies of African Americans in the U.S. Army, 1886-1917," which was based largely on government and military records, Bivins was said to have stood 5-foot-9. That book also quotes a 10th Cavalry history that said Bivins had an excellent character and a story in the Indianapolis Freeman, a newspaper, that described Bivins as "a sober, sensible, industrious Negro."

It is not clear what happened to Bivins' collection of animals and artifacts. When the Parmly Library moved out of what is now the Western Heritage Center in 1969, part of the collection was transferred to Eastern Montana College, but officials there don't know what eventually became of it.

Kevin Kooistra, deputy director of the Western Heritage Center, said there apparently are no remnants of the collection still at the center.

"I have never seen a Philippine lizard in this place," he said. "Never. We have a squirrel, but I'm pretty sure it's not from the Philippines."

One intriguing thread of Bivins' life story suggests that he may have done more in the Philippines than collect artifacts. Jess and Daniel Bevien, of the San Francisco Bay area, think Bivins had a Filipina "wife" during his years in that country and that he was their grandfather. Daniel Bevien said their father, Julian, was born in the Philippines and changed his name from Beban to Bevien sometime in the late 1940s.

"Pops did that out of the blue," Daniel said. Although there was no way of proving it, he said, "We're pretty sure he (Bivins) is our grandfather. ... My father didn't really know."

It wouldn't be very surprising if it were true, he said: "The buffalo soldiers came through the Philippines and left a lot of American kids there."

Daniel said he did enough research to convince him that Bivins was in the Philippines at the right time to have fathered Julian, but for him the best evidence came when he was touring a museum at the Presidio some years ago and saw a photograph of Horace Bivins.

"I looked at it, and I said, 'Oh, that looks like Pops,' " he said.

Jess Bevien, Julian's oldest son, said in an e-mail message that his father never saw his father, "only heard stories told to him by some of his father's compadres. My dad talked to us extensively about his life as a young man, boxer, soldier in the Philippines."

However that may be, Bivins' American family continued to live in Billings until after World War II, and Bivins was sought out now and again by reporters eager to retell his exciting story. Toward the end of the war, in a Jan. 21, 1945, article in The Gazette, Bivins told a reporter how pleased he was to have re-entered the Army during World War I.

"And I wish I was young enough for this one," he added. The same article said Bivins' wife, Claudia, had died in 1943, and one of his sons, Paul, was then stationed in the Pacific.

On Sept. 25, 1949, The Gazette wrote about Bivins again, this time to say he had recently left to live in Philadelphia, where he planned to work on a new, revised edition of "Under Fire With the Tenth U.S. Cavalry." Four days later, the Billings Herald reported that another reason for the move was that Bivins was "considering matrimony." After that the paper trail fades out. It is unknown whether Bivins ever returned to Billings or whether he died in Philadelphia.

Nor do any of the newspaper articles or books mention the fate of Booth, Bivins' celebrated Irish water spaniel. Booth was born in the West and spent his earliest days around Fort Custer. He was described as an excellent swimmer who could go against the current of the Little Bighorn River to retrieve the ducks and geese brought down by his master's gun.

In "Under Fire With the Tenth U.S. Cavalry," Booth, like Bivins, was said to have distinguished himself at the battle of San Juan Hill.

"He displayed more intelligence than is common in the animal by guarding the remains of Private Slaughter who was killed in the charge up San Juan Hill on July 1, 1898," the book says. "The dog was found lying across the dead soldier's breast."

Originally published April 13, 2003, in The Billings Gazette

HALLECK BRENDEN, R.I.P.

LAUREL — When I met Halleck Brenden back in the early 1990s, he was something of a bar-stool philosopher, always ready to embark on a rambling lecture that was a mystifying blend of genius and incoherence.

Once a woodworker and mechanic who could make or fix just about anything, Halleck used to disassemble words in a way that was almost physical, explaining what a particular root word signified in three or four languages, how it was related to similar words and how it had found its place in English.

Known to many as Fiddler, Halleck was a Montana original, a Laurel farm kid who got a degree in psycholinguistics and became a college professor on the East Coast.

He moved back to Montana for good in 1979. Ten years later, during the Great Montana Centennial Cattle Drive from Roundup to Billings, Halleck, dressed in his denim overalls and weathered leather hat, supposedly was the only person to walk the entire route. At the end of each day he was a fixture around cattle drive campfires, crooning and fiddling deep into the night.

Words were as important to Halleck as music. Even when he sang a song, either a cappella or accompanied by the fiddle he used to carry almost everywhere, he could barely get through it without pausing to gnaw on some word or phrase, puzzling out its significance or tracing its evolution.

In time, though, the bar stool grew a bit too comfortable. It was hard, even for those of us who didn't know Halleck in his prime, to watch him squander his gifts and sink into what his friend, Paul Garrison, called "a great long welter of indulgence."

And yet even at the end, when Halleck was living in a portion of an old barn on his family's property on the east end of Laurel, he was full of surprises.

The first time I went out there to see him, I thought I was visiting a virtual hermit. I quickly learned that Halleck still had a wide circle of friends, acquaintances and confidants. Men and women of all ages were always stopping by the barn, some bearing gifts and some offering him various forms of help, but many going to Halleck for advice, consolation and, if they were lucky, a song or two.

Luckily for all of us, Garrison managed to sit Halleck down last winter, five or six months before Halleck died at the age of 66, and record 13 songs and three poems, all original and all uninterrupted. The resulting CD, "Lost ... in a Honky-Tonk Dream," was recently released by Garrison, a bluesman better known by his stage name, Doctor Mongo.

Halleck, who played music his whole life and was proficient on the piano, fiddle, guitar and mandolin, sings and plays guitar on the CD. The sound that resulted, Garrison said, was old-fashioned country-western, "but the way he does it is completely Halleck." By that, Garrison said, he meant that Halleck "never aspired to be slick in the way that modern country recordings are. With Halleck, perfection was not the goal. The goal was soul. He wanted to get the feeling in the song. And that he accomplished."

He certainly did. The songs and the poems have an antique sentimentality to them, a sentimentality salvaged by sincerity. The title for the CD comes from one of Halleck's songs, "Stranger to Myself":

Well, I've always been a stranger,
The things I feel are so hard to tell.
But more and more I'm getting to be
A stranger to myself.

Since you left me, time's gone by like shadow,
Nothin's quite what it seems.
But you know where to find me, drinkin' alone,
Lost in a honky-tonk dream.

Garrison recorded the whole CD in the course of one day late last winter. He hauled his digital recording equipment and two microphones from his home in Greybull, Wyo., to the barn in Laurel. Garrison, in liner notes he wrote for the CD, said Halleck's songs "contain the very essence of the spirit of Country and Western music, sung with heartfelt emotion, self-pity and even humor, in a voice worn down by cheap cigarettes and cheaper beer."

The recording took about eight hours, Garrison said, and Halleck sang every song and recited every poem from memory. They had to back up and start a few songs over, but basically everything was done in one take, and what you hear is exactly what Garrison heard that winter day in the barn.

Halleck was playing his 50-some-year-old Gretsch, a dusty, badly battered old acoustic guitar whose strings looked as though they hadn't been changed in a decade. Garrison said he didn't dream of suggesting new strings for the recording session. The ancient strings, like Halleck's creaky voice, added to the authenticity of the music.

I never enjoyed Halleck's music more than when he would call me, during the last years of his life, to let me hear a new song. Sometimes he'd put the phone down on his bed and let loose with a song, but even better was when he'd play back a home recording over the phone, shouting out explanatory notes in the background: "Here's the bridge," "I missed that chord," "I've got to work on that line," or "I really like this part."

I wish I would reproduce some of his rambling musings on linguistic matters. He was always drunk on words, and he'd usually end his impromptu lectures with a guffaw, laughing at the odd workings of his own mind. I'm going to miss that laugh.

Fare thee well, Fiddler.

Originally published January 6, 2008, in The Billings Gazette

MARYONA JOHNSON:
SHE RAN A RESPECTABLE JOINT

The story behind this story is complicated, with connections reaching in-
to other stories past and future, but I'll try to keep it simple. I was on a
Yaak to Alzada trip with David Grubbs in 1999 when, toward the end of
our journey, we got seriously lost in ranch country southeast of Colstrip. Be-
cause we were running out of daylight, we violated our vow to avoid pavement
and larger towns, and as soon as we found the highway we headed for Miles
City. On the way there, we stopped in at the Hathaway Bar, which I had
written about many years earlier. It was an interesting place, to put it diplo-
matically, where strippers occasionally performed on a makeshift stage in the
backroom and where weary travelers (or visitors from Miles City) supposedly
could seek other comforts in the several small shacks on either side of the bar.

We stopped there hoping the proprietor could steer us in the direction of
a good story or two on the next stage of our trip to Alzada. At first, she
couldn't think of anything, but then she said, offhandedly, "Well, there is a
woman in Miles City I know. She used to be the madam at the Wild Horse
Pavilion, and now she's working as a greeter at the new Wal-Mart."

The only problem with the suggestion was that it was too good. We
knew immediately that given the scope of our current assignment, there was
no way we could squeeze such a fantastic yarn into our Yaak to Alzada se-
ries. But I tucked the name away and got in touch with Maryona a few

months later. The Wild Horse Pavilion was long gone by then, but Maryona was still living in Miles City, where she was indeed a Wal-Mart greeter. And she was only too happy to talk.

It was only after I had begun to interview her that I realized her partner in life and business, Lyle "Wild Horse" Cunningham, was one of the characters "Dobro" Dick Dillof (see Page 15) had suggested I write about years earlier. I still hadn't met Dobro Dick at that time, having only talked to him on the phone several times over the years. So, when Maryona got around to showing me a scrapbook from the Wild Horse and I saw a picture of a fellow playing the Dobro, flanked by three or four women wearing very little clothing, it didn't even occur to me it might be Dick. But Maryona pointed him out and said, "And that there is Dobro Dick." It was very strange.

One last thing: In the story, I relayed an anecdote from Maryona involving Jesse Ventura, the former wrestler who was then governor of Minnesota. After the story ran in The Gazette, a gossip columnist for the Minneapolis Star-Tribune got wind of it and wrote an item about it. Ventura's chief of staff, I think it was, wrote me a long, exceptionally rude letter, with copies sent to my editor and publisher, calling me a libeler and a hack and a miscreant who should be fired on the spot. My response consisted of one of the shortest and most satisfying letters I have ever sent. All it said was, "Dear Sir: Aw, leave me alone."

I'm glad to say that he did, and I heard nothing more of the matter. That doesn't mean I am able to vouch for the truth of the story about Jesse Ventura, but I didn't see any reason to edit it out of this version, either.

MILES CITY — Maryona Johnson was the only child of a prim and proper schoolteacher, reared on a ranch in a remote corner of Montana, north of the Milk River on the Canadian line.

She married a rancher at 18, had two children and then lost her husband in a car wreck six years into their marriage. She remarried two years later and had another child with her second husband.

Half a century later, living in an antique-filled house on Main Street in Miles City, the 77-year-old grandmother is working as a "people greeter" at the new Wal-Mart store.

But the road from the ranch to the Wal-Mart was not a straight one. It took a few turns before veering off for a long spell into what Maryona described as "the wild side of life."

The wild side included the 17 years she worked as the bartender and madam at the Wild Horse Pavilion, a saloon, strip joint and brothel that she built outside Miles City with the man she still calls her "significant other" — Lyle "Wild Horse" Cunningham.

She has countless memories of those years, and not a single regret.

She'll tell you about the hundreds of "working girls" she got to know so well, about the truckers, bikers, ranchers and cowboys who flocked to the Wild Horse for a drink and a fling. She'll talk about the doctors, legislators and lawmen who frequented the Wild Horse. She'll bend your ear about her troubles with the state, and later the IRS.

She'll even tell you about the time Lyle gave a much-needed lesson on manners to a future governor of Minnesota.

Maryona (the nickname was derived from her youthful mispronunciation of Mary Verona, her given name) said she never had any plans to go into the bordello business. She'd run a bar in Rosebud with her second husband, whom she divorced in 1960, and Lyle also had experience as a bar owner.

They decided to build a bar together in 1976, picking out a flat piece of ground eight miles northeast of Miles City, just off the interstate. They laid a 40-by-70-foot concrete foundation and brought in a load of logs from Roundup. On top of the Wild Horse Pavilion was the bar's signature feature, a big fiberglass palomino, rearing up on its hind legs.

They had live music during the first year of operation but then decided to expand the range of entertainment, based on a fact of life in that part of the world.

"Eastern Montana's always been known for a shortage of women," Maryona said. "And there were a lot of lonely men."

So she draped the bandstand in red velvet — "I went around to rummage sales and bought every red velvet curtain and bedspread in town" — and started bringing in strippers. The transition to the next level of entrepreneurship was a natural, what with all the young men on hand, and the booze, and the girls parading around without a stitch on.

It was Lyle's idea, Maryona said, and he had had some experience with brothels. In fact, he used to brag that he knew more about cathouses than any man in Miles City, a town infamous for such establishments since frontier days. He told Maryona it would be a public service and a pretty solid business proposition.

"At first, believe it or not, I was absolutely horrified," Maryona said. And she insists she had had no experience in that line of work.

"People used to say, 'You must have been a working girl yourself.' But I said, 'No.' Honest to God, I wasn't."

At first, they hauled in a trailer house and parked it behind the Wild Horse, but when it was destroyed by high winds, Lyle built a few little "cabanas" out back, Maryona said. They soon were named the Gold Room, the Blue Room and the Red Room, and the latter, with its mirrored ceiling, was a favorite. A later addition was a sheep wagon from the ranch Maryona lived in with her first husband. It was known as "The Sheepherder's Delight."

Some of the girls — Maryona always refers to them as "girls" — used to live in a trailer across the road from the Wild Horse, but later they stayed in apartments in the basement of the house Maryona and Lyle shared on Main Street.

She said the girls were under strict orders to behave themselves and they weren't allowed to go "uptown." They were checked by a doctor every week, and every three weeks they had to leave town for a while, sometimes for a couple of weeks or a month. If they stayed any longer than that at one place, Maryona said, they started getting squirrelly.

"I'll tell you," she said. "After putting up with you men, they'd get pretty short-tempered."

She usually had two or three girls working at a time, though when the Williston Basin oil boom was going strong in the early '80s she sometimes had as many as five on the roster. Maryona said she tried helping the girls, teaching them how to walk with elegance, how to dress, how to act.

"Most of 'em, I got to tell you, were more ladylike than the town girls," she said. "The town girls would come out, and their language would curl your hair."

The basic rate was $50 for a half hour, with charges added on for more time or special requests. Maryona and the girls split their earnings 50-50. The girls also got to live rent-free in the basement apartments, with doctors' visits paid for by Maryona.

Some of the girls got marriage proposals — just like in the movies — but in real life Maryona doesn't remember any of the girls ever saying yes. They were too happy with the money they were making. Sometimes the girls would try working regular jobs for a while, as barmaids or waitresses mostly, but they'd gravitate back to the Wild Horse.

"They'd call up and say, 'Mom?' — they all called me Mom — 'Can I come back? I can't live on what I make here.' "

Maryona said the Wild Horse provided a necessary service in a safe setting.

She likes to tell of the quadriplegic patron who used to drive all the way down to the Wild Horse from his place up near Wolf Point once or twice a month. He'd pull up in the parking lot, honk the horn on his van and wait for one of the girls to come out and "entertain" him.

After numerous visits, Maryona said, the man said he'd always wanted to see the inside of one of the little houses out back. So a couple of big bikers who were in the bar went out to the van, picked him up and carried him to one of the cabanas.

"He used to say, 'That's the only thing that's made life worth living, since I found this place,' " Maryona said.

"I don't think we ever hurt anybody," she said. "I really think it should be legalized, legalized and taxed like everything else."

There was rarely any trouble at the Wild Horse, Maryona said, mainly because people knew if they messed with Maryona or one of the girls, Lyle would come looking for them.

That's the way Norrine "The Outlaw Queen" Linderman remembers it, too. Norrine, a singer, guitar player, yodeler, former bar owner and longtime friend of both Lyle and Maryona, said Lyle was not known for having much patience.

"Maryona always had that nice, talkative, easy-going way about her," she said. "Lyle was the one always jumping around taking the high-spirited part of it. ... That Lyle, you know, he ran that place with an iron hand. He was big and tough if he needed to be."

Maryona will never forget one time in particular when Lyle needed to be. It was 1987 — she remembers because it was the year the Minnesota Twins won their first World Series — and a group of four or five Minnesota hunters came into the Wild Horse. One of them was a huge man with a shaved head, dressed in gray sweatpants, and his friends introduced him as a famous wrestler.

"They were very proud they brought him out, and they felt I should be impressed with him," she said.

The Minnesotans "were pretty well oiled up," Maryona said, and the big wrestler was in a belligerent mood. As soon as he came in he looked around and started talking about how he could demolish the place with his bare hands. He also grabbed one of the strippers — there were two sisters working that day — nearly pulling her off the stage.

Maryona walked out from behind the bar and asked the fellow if he was planning to cause trouble. He looked down at her and said that if he was, "a little slip of a lady" like her probably wasn't going to stop him, and that he'd have the place pulled apart before the cops could get there.

Maryona went back behind the bar and called Lyle. He drove out, slipped in the back door, sidled up to the big troublemaker and appeared to whisper something in his ear. Maryona said the 5-foot-11, 225-pound Lyle "looked like a pygmy" next to the wrestler, but he got the job done.

"I didn't know what Lyle said to him, but he just deflated," Maryona said. When Lyle came over to the bar, she asked him what he'd said. Well, he told her, he'd stuck the muzzle of a .357 Magnum pistol inside the drawstring of the wrestler's sweatpants, and threatened to shoot if he didn't behave himself.

And that wrestler, Maryona swears, was Jesse Ventura, the Reform Party governor of Minnesota.

"I have no way of proving it," Maryona said. "But I never forgot his face, or his build. ... If I'm lying, I'm dying."

Paul Moore, a spokesman in Ventura's press office, said he wouldn't bother asking the governor about the purported incident.

"I doubt he's going to take time away from governing to talk about that," Moore said.

Maryona said the only other people who could back her up are the sisters who were dancing — wherever they might be — and Lyle, who had a stroke three years ago and has been in the

Veterans Administration nursing home in Miles City ever since. Maryona warned that Lyle was in bad shape. "All he can say is 'Yes,' 'No,' and 'Goddamn,' " she said.

Lyle used most of his remaining vocabulary when he was asked if Maryona's account of the Jesse Ventura story was true. Lying in his bed at the nursing home, Lyle smiled and said, "Yes." Then he paused, smiled again and added, "Goddamn."

Maryona led a regular, proper life before meeting Lyle in 1963, shortly after divorcing her second husband.

"He was kind of a renegade," Maryona said of Lyle. "That's when I kind of drifted into the wild side of life, when I was 39."

During the '60s and '70s they often traveled to cowboy poetry gatherings, where Lyle built up a considerable following with his poems and his music. He was a good guitar player, Maryona said, and he knew all the old country and cowboy songs. He was also known as an accomplished rodeo man, picking up his "Wild Horse" handle by racing wild horses.

She wouldn't have objected to marrying Lyle, Maryona said, but every time he proposed he made a hash of it. Once he suggested they get married so the banker handling her financial affairs would have an easier time of it. She told him a man proposing to her had better do it for love, not to impress anybody else.

But Lyle asked again, after hearing that some neighbors were whispering about them, and again just before Lyle's father died. He thought his father would die happy if Lyle got married. Maryona lit into him.

"Lyle Cunningham," she said, "I wouldn't marry you to please a banker, I wouldn't marry you to please the neighbors, I wouldn't marry you to please your father. Don't you ever ask me again."

He never did, and he remains her "significant other."

Maryona said she didn't expect the Wild Horse to thrive as long as it did.

"I never thought it would last a month," she said. "I was amazed it lasted 17 years."

It probably helped that the Wild Horse was popular among some of the powers that be in the area. Maryona said a widely known banker was a regular, as were a few doctors, some state legislators and an employee of the Bureau of Alcohol, Tobacco and Firearms.

"I had a good friend who was an ATF agent, and he used to bring his boss from Washington, D.C., out there," she said.

But some people in town eventually decided to go after her — Maryona says it was all small-town politics — and wrote to the state to complain about the Wild Horse. The state began to move against her in 1991, and in February of 1992 the Montana Liquor Division of the Revenue Department pulled the club's license.

"They said I wasn't fit to own a liquor license because I had ladies of the night working out there," she said.

It wasn't long after that when Maryona ran afoul of the IRS. She said her troubles began with some misunderstandings over the sale of her old ranch in the 1970s. By the time the IRS came collecting, she said, a $15,000 discrepancy had mushroomed with interest to nearly $150,000.

The IRS seized everything — the Wild Horse, all her antiques and her personal belongings. Knowing Lyle's reputation, she said, the IRS arranged to have law officers waiting with shotguns when tax agents descended on Maryona's house.

"It took place right on Main Street," she said. "The whole town was agog."

She managed to hang on to her house and later bought back most of her antiques, but the new owner of the Wild Horse burnt the bar down. All that's left of it now is the foundation.

The final settlement with the IRS didn't come until two years ago, just about the time Maryona was hired on as one of the first "people greeters" at Miles City's new Wal-Mart store. Maryona said she took the job because she was bored and because "it's a matter of pride that I can still earn a paycheck." She didn't list any former employers on her resume, but she told the Wal-Mart folks that she'd been self-employed for years and had hired and fired hundreds of people. She didn't see any reason to go into detail.

Maryona occasionally sees some of her old customers at the Wal-Mart. A photo on her mantle shows her standing out in front of the store flanked by two burly bikers who knew her from the Wild Horse days. Other former customers are more guarded.

"Some of them do a double-take, if they're with their wives, and some of them come right up to me. It depends on the guy."

Maryona has never run from her past, and she makes no

apologies for anything she's done.

"Most farm and ranch women haven't had the pleasure and excitement I had," she said. "I wouldn't trade my life for anybody else's."

Originally published March 19, 2000, in The Billings Gazette

CHARLIE AND NOODLE

I wrote "Charlie and Noodle" as a short story many years ago, but it very nearly was a character sketch. I was one of the Missoula college kids living down the hall from Charlie in a boarding house run by his aunt, and it really was across the street from a Catholic church and school complex. The boarding house is long gone, replaced by a parking lot, and most of the other old houses on the block are gone, too.

Living in the same house as Charlie and Noodle could be a pain sometimes, but I used to love listening to their drunken patter, which I've tried to reproduce here. I seem to remember an earlier version of this story in which I had Charlie and Noodle getting into a furious argument over the correct pronunciation of the brand name on a can of pears. I don't remember why I cut it out, but it was based on a real argument they had once, and it sticks in my mind as one of the most ludicrous debates I ever heard.

Charlie was sitting in a chair near the window, sipping alternately from a can of Lucky Lager and a gold-stained old fruit jar half full of whiskey. He was in a jolly mood and singing bits and pieces from an Irish-sounding love song. The light in Charlie's room was burning, as it was always burning, day and night. He didn't sleep much and never kept regular hours, but when too much drink forced him to sleep he would climb aboard his old metal-frame bed in the corner of the room and pull the dirty, light-blue sheet up to his waist and sleep fitfully for a few hours.

He sat there staring at the blank television screen, singing softly and mumbling to himself. He heard a door open and he leaned forward to see Fisk, the old man from across the hall, going out for his daily walk. It was mid-spring and fairly warm, but Fisk had on his all-weather walking clothes: a checkered hunting cap with the ear flaps down, a worn woolen jacket, light leather gloves, heavy cotton pants, boots and his cane.

"Hi ya, Fisk," Charlie said. "Going out for a walk, eh?"

Fisk was too busy negotiating the stairs to reply, but Charlie tried again.

"Great-looking hat you've got there, Fisk."

Again Fisk said nothing, and Charlie mumbled, "You old sourpuss."

He sat back in his chair and lit another cigarette, listening to Fisk slowly making his way to the door. Then he heard another sound, of someone shuffling along the ground floor, opening and closing drawers. Charlie put his hands on either arm of his chair and tried to push himself to a standing position, but got only to where his elbows still crooked a little, and he fell back into the chair wheezing. You wouldn't have thought it would take much to hoist that gaunt frame out of a chair. He was not just skinny; he looked like the air had been let out of him. He had no backside, no gut, spindly legs and a waist so small that he had had to keep punching new holes in his worn leather belt. He waited for a few minutes, looking toward the door with an angry show of teeth. He heard someone downstairs again, and after drinking down the rest of a can of beer, eased himself slowly, slowly, to his feet. He tottered there for a moment as if ready to fall back again, but hesitantly took a step and made his way into the hall. Gripping the banister, he pushed his hair back from his forehead with his free hand and shouted hoarsely, "Hey, Noodle!"

Charlie looked over the banister, took a cigarette out of his pocket, lit it and mumbled a curse.

"Hey, Noodle!"

"OK, OK, for Christ's sake. Hold on."

Charlie turned and walked back to his room, pulled out another chair, sat down in his own and waited. After about 15 minutes he was ready to yell down the stairs again when he heard Noodle slam his door and drop something to the floor, cursing angrily. A minute later he heard Noodle coming up the stairs.

"Charlie," Noodle called. "Come here and grab this god-damn beer for me." Noodle waited midway up the stairs while Charlie worked his way to his feet once more and shuffled out to lean over the banister.

"Come up another step," Charlie said. "I'll be damned if I can reach it there."

"All right," Noodle said.

They finally made it to the room, Charlie put the six-pack on the table and they sat down heavily in their chairs.

"Christ, we're getting old," Noodle said.

"I know."

"We ain't what we used to be."

"Goddamn it, I know it, Noodle. Will you please shut up? Goddamn it."

"OK, Charlie, OK. No hard feelings. I was just talking."

"Oh, I know it, Noodle. I'm sorry. I didn't mean anything."

"Sure, all right," Noodle said. "Say how 'bout a beer. It's not too cold, but what the hell."

"Yeah, I'll take one," Charlie said. "Say, when in hell are you going to plug in your damned icebox anyway? Might as well get the power hooked up sometime."

"I'll get power just as soon as it's free, and not a minute sooner. It's bad enough a guy's got to pay for food, hell if he ought to pay to keep his body warm and his beer cold."

"Well, come on, Noodle," Charlie said with a grin. "It ain't like Uncle Sam wasn't picking up the tab. Hell, you and me have been livin' off him so long we ought to get Christmas cards this year."

"I know, Charlie, I know. But it's the principle of the thing. Besides, everybody don't have it as good as you and me. Jeez, look at Pat; she's paying through the nose with all the heat she uses, and she can't hardly afford it."

"Oh, don't bring her into this, please."

"Well, really, Charlie. How would you feel if you was her?"

"Probably a whole lot better than I feel now, and I'd stop bugging my poor goddamned nephew every five minutes. A guy should have a right to live like he wants when he gets to be my age."

Noodle looked at him and chuckled. Charlie looked at Noodle out of the corner of his eye. "What's so funny?" he asked.

"You, that's who. Carrying on and moaning as if Pat never did nothing for you. Just think where you'd be sure as hell if Pat hadn't a looked after you all these years."

Charlie didn't say anything, just picked up his fruit glass and took a sip of whiskey. He didn't put the glass down, but held it to his mouth, looking at Noodle over the tinted rim.

"Oh, yeah?" Charlie finally said quietly. "That's what you think, huh?"

Noodle didn't respond because he wasn't listening to him anymore. He was looking out the window into the street below, where a man was having a loud dispute with a meter maid. Noodle smiled a little as the man and the meter maid got more and more heated, and Noodle silently mouthed his opinion of the whole affair.

"What'd you say?" Charlie asked.

"Huh?"

"I said, what'd you say?"

"Nothing Charlie, goddamn it, nothing. I was just watching this guy down in the street bitching at a meter maid."

"Oh yeah? Well, let me have a look at this." Charlie slowly got up and went to the window and watched the two for a minute.

"Looks like there's not much getting settled down there," Charlie said. "Could be trouble."

He opened the window a few inches, stuck an empty beer can on the sill to hold it open, bent down to the opening and yelled, "Hey!" When the two looked up, he continued. "There happens to be two gentlemen up here trying to have a friendly conversation. Since you two are hollering about money, why don't you flip a goddamn coin, shake hands and get the hell out of here."

The two on the street were startled and looked at each other in their shock, though almost glad to have an enemy in common. They began to shout back in unison, but Charlie grabbed the top of the window and slammed it shut, sending the beer can spinning down to the sidewalk. He sat back down, smiled and nodded his head a few times. Noodle reached across the table and poured a finger of whiskey into Charlie's glass and then into his own. They looked at each other for a moment, raised their glasses and touched them together in a silent toast.

Noodle, whose real name was Al Padnudlen, and whose only real friend was Charlie, liked to come up to Charlie's room and drink. His ground-floor room was dark and musty, while Charlie's room, spare and dingy as it was, and permeated with grease from years of fried cooking, at least had a few big windows to let in the light.

The apartment house was one of six similar buildings lining the block, neglected and tree-shrouded old houses now mostly given over to lodging weary transients come home to rest. Across the street, rooted in the earth like ancient trees, were four other buildings — a church, a rectory, a high school and a grade school — all Catholic, all austere and foreboding. Noodle would have been hard-pressed to recall the last time his bleary eyes had seen the inside of a church, but to sit drinking beer in Charlie's room, staring out the window at that formidable row of buildings, was akin to a religious experience. The ramshackle houses facing that brick-and-granite assemblage seemed so safe, like the residents of a walled city. In his friend's room Noodle was free to sit and think — about nothing in particular, but just to sit and let the minutes tick away, watched over all the while by the same benefactors that guarded the church. Often when he and Charlie were talking, Charlie would drift off to sleep in his chair, and then Noodle would feel alone in the world, dulled by drink and with nothing more to do than watch the smoke from his cigarette curl and twine around the light above Charlie's bed.

It was late, about 2 a.m., and Charlie and Noodle were drinking a few beers together and talking. After the incident with the meter maid, Charlie had dropped off into four hours of good sleep, as if pleased with how he'd handled the whole thing. Noodle had walked down to a café on the corner for supper and then back again to his own room for a while before rejoining Charlie at about 11. From somewhere down the hall came the sounds of a radio, and they could hear the monotonous bass beat of a country song. Noodle had picked up another pint of whiskey and there was beer in Charlie's refrigerator. It was a quiet, sleepy night, punctuated by the sounds of trucks and the occasional blasts of switch engines from down in the freight yards. Charlie and Noodle were talking haphazardly, jumping from subject to subject, as if only to hear the sound of each other's voice.

"By the way, Charlie," Noodle said, "I saw an old friend of yours downtown. Frank somebody. Says he used to live next door. Wanted me to say hello."

"How'd he know you?"

"Just heard me talking, I guess."

"Yeah, Frank Rudd's his name. I don't miss the son of a bitch. He used to bum cigarettes left and right. Never seemed to have a pack of his own."

"That right?"

"Yep. Fell asleep once in my chair smoking one of my goddamned cigarettes. Started it on fire and scared the hell out of Pat. Middle of the night and the fire trucks come screaming down."

"What happened?"

"Nothing much. A guy from down the hall threw a blanket over the chair before the fire department boys got here and everybody went home. Pat told Frank to be careful and I almost slugged him. Had to throw the chair out."

"That's too bad," Noodle said. "But I know what you mean about guys like Frank. I used to be a bartender once and ..."

"Goddamn it, I know that, Noodle."

"Well, sure, Charlie. I was just saying ..."

"But goddamn it, Noodle. You didn't have to say you were a bartender. I know that."

"Damn it, Charlie, all I was saying is that when I was a bartender we always had guys like Frank come in. Always mooching."

"You think we just met? Hell, I knew you were a bartender."

"OK, OK. Christ, drop it, anyway. I remember once I went into the walk-in cooler where we kept the beer ..."

"That make sense," Charlie said.

"Right. Anyway, I was in there and I ..."

"I said it makes sense, goddamn it."

"What the hell are you talking about, Charlie? Jesus, can't I say anything?"

"I just said it made sense!" Charlie screamed, and in bringing his fist down on the table to emphasize the point, he knocked his beer to the floor.

"There you go, Charlie. Good job. You and your damned sense."

"What do you mean? Goddamn it, who started talking about …"

Suddenly a third voice, sharp and whining, cut into the room. "Chucky. It's after two o'clock. Please, couldn't you boys be a little quieter?"

It was Pat, Charlie's aunt, the landlord, who lived downstairs, peeping into Charlie's room through the rails of the banister as she stood halfway up the stairs, her thin, reddish hair tangled around her shoulders.

"Aw, Christ," Charlie mumbled.

"Hi ya, Pat," Noodle said. "Makin' too much noise, eh?"

"Yes, Al. I'm sorry boys, but you know how hard it is for me to sleep anyway, and I've got other people living here, you know."

Charlie just looked away, toward the wall, and Noodle said, "Yeah, sorry. Say, why not have a beer? It's too late to sleep now." Charlie glanced over at Pat, and seeing her standing there with her sad eyes, her bony fingers clutching the rails, he felt a rush of drunken sympathy.

"Aw, come on," he said. "Have a beer. I'm sorry we were so loud."

Pat hesitated for a moment, looked down the stairs and then back into the room.

"Well, all right. I'd probably just lay there with my eyes open anyway."

Noodle pulled out a chair for her and got a beer out of the fridge. She sat down, opened the beer, took a little sip and smiled. The three of them sat for a while in silence, listening to the radio from down the hall. A radio cowboy was singing about how his darlin' had run off and each verse of lament was answered by a harmonica, like somebody whining in the distance. Suddenly the radio was clicked off and they all looked up dreamily.

"That was nice," Pat said. "Chucky, you ought to get a radio."

"Hell," Charlie said. "It always sounds better down the hall. Can't hardly hear the commercials."

"That's right," Noodle said. "Sounds better from a ways off."

"Dick used to sing like that sometimes," Pat said sadly. "He always had a nice voice."

Dick was Pat's husband, dead 16 years but still breathing softly in her mind. It was just after he died that Charlie moved in, invited by Pat out of her loneliness and the feeling that she ought to look after him. Charlie had an honorable discharge from the Army and a 50 percent disabled rating for a bad back resulting from an injury in Korea. The government sent him barely enough money to live on and he hadn't worked a lick in 20 years. After an operation to remove part of his left lung because of cancer, he became convinced it would be best to live as inactively as possible, and gradually he had begun to drink more and more as a way of passing the time. Pat didn't like to hound Charlie about his habits, but he seemed so like a little boy to her that often she could not help herself. She watched him drink a small swig of whiskey from the old fruit glass, put her beer on the table and said, "Chucky, I don't mind you drinking beer, but that whiskey is no good. I'm not saying Dick would still be here if he hadn't drunk any, but he might have lasted a few more years."

Charlie put his hands together on the table and tilted his head down so he was looking at Pat through his eyelashes.

"Pat, why don't you leave me alone? Noodle drinks just as much as I do, but to hear you talk you'd think he was a priest. Christ, Pat, goddamn it. Leave me alone."

"Now, Chucky, don't start swearing, too. You know I love you and that's why I worry." She stopped and put a hand on Noodle's shoulder. "I love you too, Al, of course I do." Then, turning back to Charlie: "But you're like a son to me, Chucky, and I feel I have to look out for you."

"Well, why don't you just put the whole damned speech on tape and I'll listen to it a couple times a day. Save you a lot of trouble."

Pat put her other hand on Charlie's shoulder and sat there between them like an old bird with tired wings. Tears started to well up in her eyes, as they always did when Charlie got angry with her. Charlie put his cigarette out in the ashtray and reached over to give Pat a little brush on the cheek with his knuckle.

"Aw, come on, Pat. I know you love me. I guess it's just fun to get mad sometimes. Nothing else to do. I was in love once, you know."

"I know," Pat said. "That girl from Idaho. Poor girl. But I liked her. You should have married her, Chucky."

"Sure, sure. Then come back from the Army with my back like this. Hell of a husband I would have been."

"You could've gone to work," Pat said shyly. "If you hadn't started drinking so much, you ..."

"Now, Pat, don't start in," Charlie said, shaking his head slowly.

"Yes, you're right, Chucky. I'm sorry."

Noodle was beginning to feel uncomfortable and to change the subject he asked, "Say, Pat, did Fisk ever come through with the rent?"

"Oh, sure. I knew he would. He really did send his last check to his son. I saw the letter he got from him. Fisk is a nice man. I don't mind him paying late."

"You're right," Noodle said. "Fisk's a good guy."

"That wasn't a bad idea letting some younger fellows live here, either," Charlie said. "They keep the place looking all right. I saw that one college kid sweeping the stairs today."

Pat took another sip from her beer and smiled. "Yes, it was a good idea. I thought they'd be nothing but trouble, but they brighten the place up. That one, Bill, even cut down all those bushes and weeds out back so I can use the back door. I didn't figure I'd ever go out that way again."

For years Pat's apartment house had been the domain exclusively of old men and herself. But when Roger Stuart died and no old man claimed his top-floor room after two months, she rented it out to a 19-year-old university student. After that she eventually let out three more rooms to young men, and then the little house out back that she owned, too. Having the young men around made it nice on Charlie, Noodle, Pat, Fisk and Jack Bowman, the retired brakeman who lived in the front room downstairs. The young men helped keep up repairs and were usually willing to stop in and listen awhile to the reminiscences of the old-timers.

"I'm even thinking of getting a couple of them to paint the

outside of the house," Pat said. "It would sure look nice."

"I don't know," Charlie said. "Painting costs some money."

"Sure it does, but it would look nice. Being right across from the church and all, I think maybe it would be a good idea."

"I painted a few houses when I was younger," Noodle said, scratching his sparse gray beard. "It's not bad work if you lay in a few cases of beer and don't worry about how long it takes."

"I helped my uncle paint a house once," Charlie said. "He had a big damn place in Miles City. I got paint all over the windows and he acted like he'd have to buy a new house. That son of a bitch."

"Now, Chucky, don't you talk like that about your relatives. Your Uncle Jim was a good man and he always treated your Aunt Kate just fine."

"That may be, but goddamn it, I wasn't a professional. And he wasn't paying me hardly anything at all."

Noodle got up and went to the fridge for another beer. "Need another one, Charlie? How 'bout you, Pat?" Charlie nodded his head as he finished his beer, but Pat shook her head and said, "No, thanks, Al. One is plenty. You know what beer does to me."

"Come on, Pat. One more isn't going to put you in your grave."

Charlie let out a short laugh and Pat allowed herself to smile.

"Well, OK. But after this one I'm going to bed."

They sat and drank for another half hour, interrupting one another's idle daydreams from time to time to tell a few stories. Noodle talked Pat into having another beer, and it was when that one was half gone that she began to get a little tipsy, sitting there with her hands folded and her elbows on her knees, looking wistfully at the old tile beneath her feet and talking softly about things she and Dick had done together. She was describing a picnic they'd had on the Missouri River when she began to cry a little, wiping the tears back with her old hand and then drying it on her bath robe. Charlie reached over and put his gnarled hand on her back and tapped it softly. "That's OK, Pat. You still got me and Noodle. We ain't as good as Dick, not by a long shot, but we'll take care of you."

That cheered her a bit and she looked up to see Noodle nodding warmly.

"That's right, Pat. Me and Charlie are here, and now all these college kids. You'll do all right."

"I know," Pat said, smiling through her tears. "But damn it — excuse my language — Dick was a good one and I do miss him some nights."

"Sure you do, Pat, sure you do," Charlie said. "And that's all right. Only don't forget who your friends are. Hell, I got to admit it. You been damned good to me and who knows where I'd be if you hadn't a invited me down."

"Thanks, Charlie. That's nice. You get to be my age and you like to hear that kind of stuff sometimes."

"Well, it's true. Without you and Noodle …" Charlie paused and looked at Noodle, feeling a little embarrassed. He'd never really spoken of their friendship before, but now with Pat and her tears and nostalgia, it just slipped out. Noodle lowered his head and looked at the floor. The three of them sat there quietly for a few minutes, until Noodle broke the spell to say, "Well, you two, I guess we could all use some sleep. I think I'll hit the hay."

To her surprise, Pat found herself saying, "Oh, Al, it's too late now. We might as well sit here for a while longer." Charlie and Noodle grinned at each other across the table.

"Yeah," Charlie said. "Pat's right. No sense rushing things."

So they sat and sat and talked and talked and Pat had yet another beer; too much, really, for her. Noodle was talking about his first wife, and the little house they shared in Minnesota, and Charlie was listening with a dumb, drunken amusement. In the middle of the story, Pat suddenly cut in and said in a determined voice, as if she'd been rehearsing her lines, "Charlie, you drink too much whiskey. Between that and the cigarettes it's a miracle you're still here." Noodle tried to continue his story, but it was too late. Charlie took a slow, calculated sip of whiskey and said, "Pat, there's nothing wrong with whiskey. You just have to know how to take it. I think it's damned good for you if you want to know the truth."

"Good for you? Chucky, I hope you're joking. The devil distills that stuff and you take it in like a sponge."

"Oh, a sponge, eh? I know how to handle it. You don't know me."

"Charlie …" Noodle said.

"I don't know you?" Pat cut in. "I don't know you? I know you inside and out and sometimes I think you're trying to kill yourself."

"Kill myself? Are you crazy? I'd just stick my head in the oven and you'd read about it in the paper. Whiskey ain't bad."

"Look at yourself. Look at yourself in the mirror. Sixty-three years old and you can't hardly get out of that chair."

"It's my goddamned back and you know it. I served my country and what do I get? An old aunt treating me like a kid with his pants on backwards." They were being cruel to each other, but the argument pulled them along, against their wills.

"It isn't your pants that are on backwards," Pat shouted. "It's your head. You think you're so smart."

"Smart? Who's doing all the preaching? I was just sitting here listening to Noodle." At the mention of his name, Noodle thought he could still save the situation, but before he opened his mouth Pat was back at it.

"Charlie, I don't know why I let you live here. All I do for you and then you just sit here day after day drinking whiskey and mumbling."

"I don't drink whiskey every day. Me and Noodle just break out a pint every now and then." He looked to Noodle for support, but Noodle looked away, knowing he'd lose no matter what he said.

Pat said, "Every now and then, huh? Must be a lot of holidays or something. Seems to me you're always at the whiskey."

"So what if I am?"

"So, it's going to kill you and in the meantime you're no good. Always drunk and bothering your poor old auntie."

Charlie picked up a bent, dirty fork and waved it in front of Pat's face.

"Bothering my old auntie, eh? Poor old auntie." Charlie let out a grunt and threw the fork against the wall. It hit his shaving mirror propped up in the soap dish above the sink and the mirror went crashing down into the porcelain. The sound seemed to bring Charlie to his senses and he looked sadly at Pat, who was just beginning to sob dryly, her chin fallen against her chest. "Oh, Chucky, Chucky, why do you do it?"

She got up slowly, uncertainly after all that beer, and went to the sink, bending over to look at her scattered reflection in the broken bits of mirror. She reached down to pick up some of the shards of glass, but she lost her balance. With one hand she stopped her fall against the stove pipe, and the other hand fell into the sink. She caught the third finger of her left hand on a large piece of glass and brought it up with a jerk to eye level. It was bleeding big red drops of blood, falling onto her bath robe, her slippers and the floor.

"Oh, Charles," she said with a sob. "See what you did?" With the blood still dripping, she ran out of the room. Charlie and Noodle moved to follow her, but Charlie got up too fast and fell to the floor, landing on his back. He groped around until he reached his bed, and he lifted himself painfully to a sitting position, his back propped against the bed, both elbows resting on the mattress, but he could get no farther. Noodle ran after Pat and caught her arm as she rounded the banister. He held her arm gently and stroked her hair, helping her down the stairs and muttering, "It's all right, Pat. It's all right."

Charlie could hear them down in Pat's room, talking excitedly and rummaging around, evidently in search of something to stop the bleeding. He felt too weak and too guilty to call for help himself. He waited a few more minutes, until he could no longer hear them. Taking a deep breath, meaning to yell down, he opened his mouth but managed only a short, soft, "Hey."

He tried again a minute later, somewhat louder, but still he heard nothing from downstairs. Then one of the young men suddenly appeared in the room, fumbling with the belt on his pants and asking if everything was all right.

"I heard some noise a while ago. What happened?"

"Nothing," Charlie said. "Nothing. Pat cut herself and I fell on the floor."

The kid was helping Charlie back into his chair, Charlie grumbling, "Easy, easy," when Charlie saw Pat and Noodle in the stairwell, looking at him through the rails. He made a waving motion with his hand and the kid, looking behind him and seeing the two of them hovering out there, helped Charlie to a sitting position and left the room amid mumbled thanks from Charlie. Pat and Noodle stood there in the doorway, Noodle looking at his feet and Pat holding her wounded finger to her bosom. It was wrapped in a white towel soaked reddish-copper with iodine and blood. They stared back and forth for a long time, and Charlie finally managed a weak smile.

"Well," he said, smiling like a schoolboy caught cheating. "Well."

Pat tried to look angry, but seeing Charlie sitting in his chair with his legs splayed out in front of him and his arms just barely providing enough support, she smiled faintly and looked to Noodle. He helped her to the table and they both sat down.

"You OK?" Pat asked.

"Sure, I'm fine. How are you?"

"I'm OK. It's just a small cut, really. Lots of blood was all."

Dawn was just breaking and a few feeble streaks of light caught the leaves of the trees lining the street. Pat looked out the window and said, "Sure you're OK? I heard you fall."

"Don't worry about me," Charlie said, trying to look brave.

"You probably don't feel so good," she said. "How 'bout a little whiskey? I could use a shot myself."

"All right," Charlie said, "but only just a little. It's morning and I shouldn't drink so much."

Noodle picked up the whiskey bottle and held it to the window and they all watched as it caught a glint of sunlight.

"Looks pretty damn empty," he said.

Pat and Charlie looked at the bottle and then at each other and shared a dry laugh.

"I really ought to get my own radio," Charlie said. "Then at least I could hear it when I want to."

Previously unpublished

VINCE STAIMINGER:
ARSENIC EATER

ANACONDA — When you listen to Vince Staiminger recount the story of his life, it's a good idea not to start worrying about dates, locations or chronology. He is an encyclopedia of stories, tales and anecdotes, and of what Mark Twain called "stretchers," but his encyclopedia is not in alphabetical order and there is no index.

He just starts to talk, and as he does so his faded blue eyes begin to waver, one recollection calling up another until 90 years of memories weave and mingle and join together.

One afternoon, Vince called the Anaconda office of The Montana Standard, gave his name, announced that he was 90 years old and tendered a simple invitation: "Come on up and I'll tell you some stories." A few afternoons later, sipping a beer and chewing his Peerless tobacco as he sat inside the screened front porch of his house a little west of Anaconda, Vince did just that. His stories jump back and forth over the decades, and most of them are related to the staggering number of jobs he's held. A listener occasionally stops to pin down a date, and Vince leans back for a moment, thinking. Then, suddenly, he is off again on a different tale and the question is forgotten forever.

One thing he does remember clearly is that he was born on Jan. 22, 1891, on the top floor of a flour mill in the town of Vrbousko, Croatia, in Yugoslavia. When he was 5 or 6 he joined several cousins on a voyage to Pittsburgh, where his father, who had already worked in Colorado and Brazil, was a foreman in a steel mill.

But Vince has few memories to relate from his childhood. His story really begins when he went to work for the New York Standard Cable Co. at about age 14. The company was laying several miles of underground cable, and Vince's job was to stand at various manholes with a flag, trying to keep pedestrians above ground. That same year he hired on as a core maker in a Pittsburgh foundry, but he soon quit because "they only was paying 35 cents a hundred. We didn't do very good."

By the time he was 16 or 17, he had gone through a succession of part-time jobs and was ready to travel. He hopped a Baltimore & Ohio Railroad boxcar and headed out west. The first stop was Missouri, where Vince worked at a sawmill tending horses, which he recalls as "the best job I ever had to do nothing." When doing nothing got old, he moved on to Arkansas and signed on with a traveling Wild West show as a stage carpenter. The show made a few circuits through Arkansas and then swung down through Texas and New Mexico. "Then they wanted to go to South America from New Mexico and I wouldn't go. I quit 'em."

He doesn't remember how he landed his next job, but he knows he was a cook on a cattle drive down to San Antonio. He sums up his recollections of that period by saying, "Three times a day. Hot biscuits, fat meat and sorghum. I threw in the red beans for nothing. That country was lousy with red beans."

When the cattle drive ended he hopped aboard another boxcar, called on a few acquaintances in Louisiana and rolled into Warren, Ark., on Christmas Day, where he went to work for his uncle making barrel staves. Next it was back to Pittsburgh for a while, until he was infected with wanderlust again and hit the rails heading west, accompanied by a friend named John Proxell. They worked for a time in a tobacco factory in St. Louis, then headed north, through Minnesota, North Dakota and into Montana, where they found jobs unloading coal cars in Roundup.

Vince remembers stopping in Butte for the first time and sleeping in a graveyard — "one gravestone for the pillow, one for the feet." When they rolled into Anaconda they had $40 each left from the Roundup job and they were feeling pretty good. They spent about a month in town before Proxell decided he was going back to Pittsburgh.

Vince, however, had made a decision. He told his friend, "I'm going to stay here and drink clear Montana water. I like the good water and good air."

His first job in Anaconda was working up on "the hill," at the Anaconda Copper smelter, in the arsenic refinery. Despite his fondness for clean air, Vince says the hill was so thick with poisonous dust that "I used to eat a teaspoon full of arsenic every day to keep from dying." Asked if everyone else on the hill followed the same regimen, Vince said, "Any of 'em didn't eat arsenic, he's down six foot. It's an old saying: 'Cure a poison with a poison.' "

He worked on the hill three or four months and then found a job building a road out to Gregson. When that ended he worked as a blacksmith and wagon maker for several years, going from farm to farm in the Deer Lodge Valley. He's not sure when he worked at a couple of dozen other jobs, but he remembers the details of each. One of them involved walking from department to department at the smelter, winding clocks. The smelter complex was so huge and there were so many clocks that when you wound the last one, the first one needed winding already. He called it "the worst job a man could have."

He recalls being summoned to Deer Lodge once to repair a tractor that no one else could fix, and getting paid $200 for his successful effort. And there was a job on a Forest Service lookout up the Big Hole, where he also built a 36-bunk barracks for firefighters. He drove a horse-drawn ambulance on the hill for a while, was a switchman on the local tram, and worked at the smelter in a mill, in one of the roasters and for a time on the coal pile.

When he wasn't working, Vince managed to stay busy, too. In 1919 a "shotgun marriage" united him with a woman whom he divorced shortly after their only child, a daughter, died at age 2. He met his current wife, Marie, through correspondence. She was living in Rockford, Ill., and the two wrote back and forth for almost a year before Vince proposed. Sight unseen, Marie came out in 1952, when she was 41 and he was 61. "I've never been sorry a day," she says now.

Vince also has a good collection of bootlegging stories, about how he had a still in a chicken coop down the road from his house, and three or four more at different times in the hills south of Anaconda. He swears "there's whiskey buried up in them hills yet," and he gives cryptic directions regarding an 80-gallon barrel still buried "under a fence."

He retired from the smelter in 1958 and since then, he says, he has devoted himself to "peddling the bull." He was in the hospital recently, but he says he's feeling better now. For a 90-year-old man, he still gets around quite well. Asked for his prescription for a long and healthy life, Vince replied without hesitation: "Eat lots of arsenic."

Originally published August 26, 1981, in The Montana Standard

BEHOLD, THE PETRIFIED MAN

If nothing else, the owners of a Montana marvel known as "the petrified man" were good at advertising their product. "The wonder of the century," they called it, and they rounded up purported doctors and dentists who testified that it was a genuine human being that had somehow turned to stone.

A postcard from the early 1900s advertising the curio included quotes from Dr. S.E. Schwartz ("A most remarkable curiosity and absolutely authentic") and Dr. Donald D. Campbell ("I have examined the petrified man and consider it a genuine specimen and a wonder"). The owners hit on an even better selling point when they began identifying the specimen as the petrified remains of Thomas Francis Meagher, an Irish revolutionary, Civil War general and acting governor of Montana Territory at the time of his death in 1867.

In 1899 and on into the early 1900s, the petrified man was displayed all over Montana at 25 cents a gawk, bringing in thousands of dollars. It was also seen, somewhat less enthusiastically, in Chicago and New York. Much was written about the curiosity in its heyday, but the two questions most likely to be asked by anyone interested in the petrified man nowadays — was it real and where did it end up? — remain unanswered.

A man named Tom Dunbar claimed to have found the petrified body in the Missouri River a little downstream of Fort Benton in 1897. The river level was low and the body was underwater, half buried in sand, Dunbar later told a New York newspaperman. Dunbar said he pulled the body out of the river with a rope, and having no wagon then, buried it in the sand well away from the river until he could come back for it, which he did 18 months later. He immediately took to exhibiting the petrified man to tourists in Yellowstone National Park.

A reporter for the Bozeman Chronicle, in an article published Sept. 7, 1899, filed a story after viewing the remains. He said he knew the body was petrified because "the owner took a club and biffed it over the body with a resounding whack." It was also in September of that year that Dunbar sold the petrified man to Arthur Wellington Miles, a nephew of Gen. Nelson A. Miles, for whom Miles City was named. A.W. Miles, a Livingston businessman and former mayor of that town, wasted no time capitalizing on his investment. He began by displaying the petrified man, reclining in a pine coffin, in a vacant building near his lumberyard. The Great Falls Tribune reported on Oct. 3 that the curio was attracting big crowds and that receipts "have not yet fallen below $60 per day." That would convert to nearly $1,500 in today's dollars.

The petrified man was exhibited throughout Western Montana and eastern Washington in the last months of 1899, so successfully that Miles and his partners began to dream of bigger things — taking the petrified man by train to New York, with stops along the way in St. Paul, Chicago and other cities. No previous attempts at identifying the petrified man had been made to this point, but with the prospect of an Eastern tour in mind, Miles suddenly "recollected" what a miner who viewed the specimen in Butte (or Anaconda, according to one source) had said regarding it.

An article published in the New York World on Dec. 31, 1899, with a Butte dateline, reported that the miner, viewing the remains, exclaimed, "It is the General — God rest his soul! It is the General!" Asked what general he was referring to, the old miner replied, "Gen. Meagher, surely! If that is not the hand of Thomas Francis Meagher, may mine be withered!" Saying which, he pointed to "a slight peculiarity" of Meagher's hand, which was not further explained.

The story stuck, mainly because Meagher, acting governor of Montana Territory at the time of his death, expired close to where the petrified man was found. Meagher was on a steamboat at the Fort Benton levee when he stumbled, dived or was pushed over the rail into the Missouri River on the night of July 1-2, 1867. There was a hole in the petrified man's skull. Originally thought to have been a bullet hole, it was now said to have been caused by an arrowhead, and his hands were bound in thongs of leather, also petrified. As one theory ran, Meagher was killed by Indians — no one hearing the silent arrow — who dragged him out of the river, bound his hands and then, "alarmed at the commotion" made by Meagher's friends on the steamboat, threw him back in the water.

There he sat, somehow becoming petrified at the bottom of the river, until Dunbar found him 30 years later.

Armed with this new legend, the owners of the petrified man looked forward to his grand tour. When the procession started east in December 1899, Miles and his partners were briefly alarmed by an incident in Billings, where the pioneer scout and Indian fighter "Liver Eatin'" Johnston was brought to view the petrified man. According to an undated article from an unnamed newspaper, found in the archives of the Overholser Historical Research Center in Fort Benton, Johnston took one look at the stone man, described as the "stellar curiosity of the day," and said, "Hully gee! I knew that fellow 25 years ago. That's Antelope Charley!" Johnston then went on to explain, in great detail, how Antelope Charley had gone off with 10 barrels of whiskey to trade with Indians below Fort Benton and had apparently lost both his investment and his life at the hands of his prospective clients.

Miles and his associates did all they could to quash this new theory, and they worked hard to publicize the Eastern tour and the connection with the Irish hero Meagher. Antelope Charley was soon forgotten, but in any guise the petrified man did not stir much interest in Chicago and New York. The late historian Dave Walter, in his book "Montana Campfire Tales," said revenue from the New York showing in January 1900 "totaled less than the incurred expenses."

The petrified man continued to be shown sporadically in Montana. Laura Steinmetz of Laurel owns a postcard, apparently dating to the early 1900s, advertising an exhibit of "A Great Wonder, a Petrified Man," at an undisclosed location. It tells how he was pulled from the Missouri and exhibited in Yellowstone Park, but there is no mention of Gen. Meagher. An ad for the "Wonder of the Century, the Petrified Man" appeared in the Anaconda Standard in 1910, and on Sept. 20, 1922, the Billings Gazette ran a vertical photo of the "Petrified Man Snapped in Repose," which was then on display at the Midland Empire Fair Grounds. A part of the caption read: "Educational exhibit for ladies, gentlemen and children, nature's masterpiece."

Walter said A.W. Miles sold the petrified man "just after World War I." He also said that Daniel N. Miles, A.W.'s son, re-called seeing the specimen at a later date, when the buyer exhi-bited him in a trailer. That buyer subsequently sold the curiosity to another showman, and the Miles family lost track of him. An article from the Helena Daily Independent, dated Sept. 28, 1922, said the owner of the petrified man at that point was V.M. King, of whom nothing else is known. That article and many others were unearthed by Ken Robison, a historian at the research cen-ter in Fort Benton.

Stan Todd of Livingston, Daniel N. Miles' stepson, never saw the petrified man himself, and he regrets that he didn't listen more closely to his father's stories when he was young. He does recall that the thing "was quite a novelty," and as far as he re-members, his father considered it a hoax.

When Montana: The Magazine of Western History wrote about the petrified man in its Winter 1962 edition, the wherea-bouts of the petrified man were unknown. The last sentence read: "If any of our readers can provide further clues, let us hear them."

Meanwhile, the big question remains: What exactly was the thing advertised as the petrified man? None of the contemporary articles takes a stab at an answer. Even the stories that poked fun at the marvel made no attempt to say what it actually was. Mon-tana: The Magazine of Western History quoted an anthropologist with the Smithsonian Institution who said "there are no reliably reported instances of human flesh that has become fossiled."

Tom Roll, a professor emeritus in the Department of Sociology and Anthropology at Montana State University Bozeman, said the petrified man was most likely a simple hoax. He said petrification involves the replacement of the original material — bones, say, or wood — by silica, and it is "extremely doubtful that fleshy human remains would survive to be petrified."

Randall Skelton, a forensic anthropologist at the University of Montana, concurred in calling it a hoax. It has never been shown that a human body could petrify, he said, though there are cases of fat being converted to a soap-like substance called adipocere. This occurs in wet environments, and there is at least one case of minerals from the soil permeating the adipocere and making it harder, he said. Roll also mentioned the Bog People of England, whose fleshy parts were preserved in an anaerobic environment. But the Fort Benton petrified man was apparently hard as stone, and advertisements said the 5-foot, 10-inch specimen weighed 365 pounds.

Other evidence of a hoax is that the Montana petrified man was hardly the only such curiosity in the 1800s and early 1900s. The famous Cardiff Giant, found on a farm near Cardiff, N.Y., in 1869, caused a sensation for many years and made a fortune for its owner, George Hull. He later admitted having hired men to carve the 10-foot giant out of a block of gypsum.

Similar hoaxes were common in the West. In 1862, a young Mark Twain wrote an article for the Territorial Express in Virginia City, Nev., about the discovery of a petrified man. Twain later admitted that he fabricated the story in hopes of ending the public's fascination with such hoaxes. "One could scarcely pick up a paper without finding in it one or two glorified discoveries of this kind," Twain wrote. "The mania was becoming a little ridiculous. ... I chose to kill the petrification mania with a delicate, a very delicate satire."

His satire proved too subtle. The article was widely reprinted, only adding to the mania.

Originally published March 14, 2009, in The Billings Gazette

STRANGE DOINGS AT TWO MOON PARK

This piece might look like a strange thing to have run in a newspaper, so let me explain. My daughter and I, on an outing at Two Moon Park, discovered all of the odd things mentioned in the story, and the more we talked about them, inventing ridiculous explanations for how they came to be, the more I wanted to write something about them.

My editors indulged me, though I think they must have wondered what they were getting themselves into. Best of all, the public officials I interviewed all got it almost immediately. That is, they understood that I was writing a deliberately ludicrous story without my having to tell them so, and all of them played along, serving up the quotes without which the story would not have been half as good. I was uneasy at the time and I'm still a little uneasy when I think of how many readers thought I was serious, but I loved getting something so weird into the newspaper. And my daughter was thrilled.

BILLINGS — Several mysterious, not to say frightening, objects found in Two Moon Park could be evidence of extraterrestrial visitation, or possibly of the existence of devil worshippers, The Billings Gazette has learned.

It is possible, of course, that the artifacts in question are nothing more than highly imaginative, ad hoc public art projects created by park visitors under the powerful influence of the area's natural beauty. But this reporter sees no reason to pursue that humdrum possibility.

No, in the absence of any indication of what the objects are being used for, or who created them, it seems better to open the door to rampant speculation.

What exactly are these strange artifacts?

One of them is a wall about 12 feet long, made of sandstone and shale slabs, at the downstream end of Two Moon Park. The elaborately constructed wall, with a doorway in the middle, serves no apparent purpose and runs between the face of a steep cliff and a large concrete cylinder at the edge of the Yellowstone River.

Another is a corral-like enclosure about 10 feet in diameter made of branches, each one carefully stripped of bark, fitted one into another by means of painstakingly bored holes and carved, tapered ends. There is no gate on the corral, just an opening topped by a wooden arch.

Lastly, not far from the corral, in a shallow ravine thickly shrouded by Russian olive trees, is an abandoned GE washing machine, bent, battered and rusted, with a stout length of wood extending up from it. On top of the piece of timber is a small plastic figure of Spider-Man, his arms and legs wound about with layers of tinfoil and duct tape.

There could well be more and even stranger artifacts in the park, the entrance to which is just beyond Centennial Arena, but these are the only ones to have come to light thus far. There is no evidence to suggest that these artifacts or installations are being used by groups of devil worshippers, and nothing that points to the involvement of extraterrestrial visitors.

Still, there is no conclusive evidence that the objects are not being used for devil worship.

Norm Schoenthal, the caretaker of Two Moon Park, was receptive to the possibility that the strange doings in Two Moon Park were somehow connected to people practicing Druidism, a possibility suggested by this reporter.

"It's got to be Druids," Schoenthal said. "That'd be perfect."

As for extraterrestrial visitors, "Chariots of the Gods?" author Erich von Daniken long ago argued convincingly that most of the myths, arts and social organizations of ancient civilizations were introduced by travelers from other worlds. Could these ancient astronauts be visiting our planet again?

Cal Cumin, administrator of the Yellowstone County Park Board, said he hadn't seen any of the artifacts and had not heard of any gatherings of strange folk in Two Moon Park. He did say, when told of the Spider-Man figure, "that's pretty strange."

He also revealed that when he was a boy, a young "hellion" of his acquaintance had a hideout — a cave covered by a piece of plywood — in Two Moon Park. The young hellion, Cumin continued, also drove numerous railroad spikes into a tall cottonwood tree, which he would then climb in order to look out over the park.

It was unclear whether Cumin intended to imply that there was any connection between the hellion and the recent strange sightings.

Schoenthal, for his part, likewise claimed to have no knowledge of the stone wall, the wooden corral or the Spider-Man figure in the washing machine.

"I'll be damned," he said, when told of them. "I've got to get down there."

The wooden corral is located about a quarter-mile from the Two Moon parking lot, just off the Dull Knife Trail, one of four marked paths running through the park. The corral — or the holding pen for victims of satanic sacrifice, as it may be — gives every evidence of prolonged and committed labor, and the observer is left to ponder, why? Why?

In the river silt all around the corral there are numerous tracks, some of them obviously left by human beings, some by dogs and some by creatures perhaps unknown to science.

As for the Spider-Man figure, the only other detail worth mentioning is that he is wearing a duct-tape garment around his waist, a kind of Sumo-wrestler-like diaper. The significance of the garment is not known.

Most intriguing of all is the stone wall at the downstream end of the park. The long, heavy slab used to form the opening in the wall looks too large to have been put there by human beings.

Similarly, just beyond the wall, forming a kind of walkway, are three or four extremely heavy slabs. One is tempted to conclude, as von Daniken did in the case of Stonehenge and the statues at Easter Island, that they were moved into place by alien visitors.

Yellowstone County Sheriff Chuck Maxwell professed to have heard no reports of devil worship or ETs in the park.

He did sound surprised to hear about the unsettling objects discovered at Two Moon, however, and when asked whether he was prepared to state categorically that the objects had nothing to do with either aliens or followers of the Dark Lord, Maxwell said, and we quote:

"At this point I'm not ruling anything out."

Originally published January 8, 2003, in The Billings Gazette

GARNET STEPHENSON:
A WRITER

WEST OF ANACONDA — It's been just about 46 years since Garnet Stephenson moved away from the family homestead on the dry rolling plains north of Forsyth, but in a way she never really left. Almost everything about her, from her beliefs, ideas and morals to the very house she lives in, seems to hark back to those stern, simple days when her family tried to scratch out a living in Eastern Montana.

And when she turned to writing in her mid-40s, rediscovering a joy that she had almost ignored since early childhood, her stories, poems and musings were stamped with the old-fashioned sensibilities of the frontier. In her historical and fictional pieces, many of which have appeared in magazines and newspapers or which she has published herself in small booklets, good triumphs over evil, bad men come to bad ends and God inevitably rewards the just. Her poems reflect a deep attachment to the land, and a deep love of Montana, and she is given to moralistic ponderings on the fate of a confusing and sometimes appalling modern world.

She is also a prodigal writer of letters to the editor. Regular readers of the Montana Standard, Philipsburg Mail and Anaconda Leader are accustomed to her confident pronouncements on dozens of timely issues.

"I've spouted off on many things over the years," she says, "but I guess I'm just pioneer spirit enough, and American spirit enough, to not go along with a lot of what's going on." She says she realizes that many people think she and her husband, Paul, are "crackpots," but she is undaunted and proudly admits that "we march to a different drummer."

Garnet was born on Dec. 6, 1919, to Eli and Lillian Coole, the seventh of nine children. In her early years the whole family lived in a long, two-room house on a dryland homestead near Forsyth. Her father was crippled by arthritis and walked with two canes as long as Garnet could remember, so there was plenty of work from dawn to dusk for her mother and all the children. It was a life that didn't differ greatly from that of the first homesteaders in Montana. Garnet tells of churning butter, milking cows, harnessing horses and, later on, using an old hand-crank telephone that relied partly on barbed-wire fences for transmission. She can hardly begin to talk about those times without tears coming to her eyes, so she cuts her recollections short and says simply, "They were just plain hard years."

She wrote her first poem in the third grade but came in for such a round of ridicule that for the next 40 years, "if I wrote anything, I hid it. Tore it up or hid it, one or t'other." Still, she says, "I've always wanted to write. From the time I was little I always went around reciting poetry. ... In school I usually had the poems memorized before the rest of the students got to them."

She married Paul Stephenson in 1936. He had grown up on a homestead not far from Garnet's family, and she had known him all her life. They moved to the Livingston area soon after their marriage, driven from Forsyth, as Garnet says, "by drought and depression." They stayed there for 19 years before moving to Echo Lake, west of Anaconda, in 1955. Then, about 12 years ago, Garnet got her first good look at a long, narrow, two-acre parcel of land alongside Warm Springs Creek, about eight miles west of Anaconda.

"I stood there and looked at it and fell in love with it. I prayed we could have it and live out our lives there."

It wasn't long before her dream came true. In 1970, they moved to the land and into the log cabin built in 1912 by Abe

Larivee. The three-room cabin now is just about as homey as a house can be, adorned with antiques, Paul's woodcarvings, Indian artifacts and an ancient "Home Comfort" wood stove. Foster Creek forms the western border of their property and Warm Springs Creek ripples along the whole southern edge. The two acres are covered with chicken coops, an old storehouse, a greenhouse and a root cellar, patches of garden and jumbled bunches of fencing, prancing hens and a dozen sheep.

Garnet can tell you the history of nearly everyone who lived on that land, and the histories of many people in the surrounding area. She had long been in the habit of searching out historical tidbits and stories of Montana's past, but it wasn't until she was in her 40s that she started thinking of putting them down on paper. A friend told her that the seventh child is often specially gifted in some way and that God had given Garnet a talent for writing, which she should take care not to waste.

Her first book, "Snows of Echo Lake," was a factual narrative of the area, stretching from the days of the first white man to those of contemporary lakeside residents. After that book was published in 1966, she began writing in earnest, turning out four more volumes and countless poems in the next 15 years. Her longest book is "Pine City, Montana Territory," the story of a fictional mining camp presided over by a simple, goodly man of the cloth, "Preacher Bud."

The writing is direct and straightforward and the turns of plot are sometimes rather abrupt, but it captures the spirit of those early days and is based on long hours of talking with old-timers and poring through books and newspaper files. Her poems, too, are often grounded in history, but usually they are just paeans to the land and lifestyle she has come to love. She can recite a good many of her poems, and when she does so she closes her eyes, crosses her arms, leans her head back and pours forth the lines in an almost Irish lilt, a style perfectly suited to her simple, always rhyming verses. When asked, for instance, how she compares the eastern and western areas of Montana, she squeezes her eyes shut, pauses for breath and recites a poem, which begins:

I who saw the thirties

In east' Montana land
Do welcome most the showers that fall
On Rocky Mountains Grand.

Part of Garnet's intense interest in history stems from the deep roots her family has cast down in America, where both her paternal and maternal relations settled before the Revolutionary War. Garnet is a mixture of Scots-Irish, Pennsylvania Dutch, German, "melting-pot New Englander" and a touch of Narragansett Indian. She readily acknowledges, though, that whatever talent she has comes from God, and in the introductions to four of her books, she gives thanks to "The Mighty One Above."

She says her parents were "decent Christian people," but not overly religious. She refers to herself as "an undenominational Protestant," in much the same way she refuses to pin an identifying tag on her politically conservative beliefs. All her writings are laced with biblical references and heavy doses of fundamentalist morality, and in her letters to the editor the influence of the devil is a recurring theme.

"That old boy Satan has a pretty good hold on this world," she says. "I've often asked — could it have been any worse before the Flood?"

She reads one or two chapters from the Bible every day in the winter and is fond of quoting from Revelation concerning the demise of a sinful world. Garnet's eyes are going bad and she has pretty much given up writing, except for the letters to the newspapers, which she feels moved to compose at least once a month. She is also an amateur photographer and has put together a scrapbook of pictures and accompanying poems, which she hopes to have published someday.

In the meantime, with all four children out on their own and the first great-grandchild about to join six grandchildren, she and Paul have settled into a comfortable routine at their little homestead. She describes her feelings in a poem titled "My Paradise."

Give me a rippling creek, Dear Lord
With pine trees 'long the shore.
Let the mountains rise around me
And I'll ask but little more.

Only a comfy little cabin
And a fire to sit beside,
Food and raiment for our needs
And a bed at eventide.

Some friends to come and visit
And drop by for a chat,
A picnic in the summer;
I've always time for that.

Some letters from our loved ones
Who have now grown tall and wise,
A few good books to read, Lord
And I have my paradise.

Originally published July 18, 1982, in The Montana Standard

JIM FRIGO, R.I.P.

BILLINGS — Even on his deathbed, Jim Frigo had one last surprise for his friends.

The intensely private musician who so rarely talked about his personal life was lying unconscious and on morphine, having suffered a serious head injury in a fall down a flight of stairs. For the first time in anyone's memory, he wasn't wearing a hat.

There were a few wisps of long, white hair curling around his bald pate, but from the back of his head there grew a single dreadlock, which he must have kept tucked under his hat during all his years in Billings. The dreadlock, which none of his friends had ever seen, stretched all the way down to his waist.

"There was a majesty about it, like a Viking lying in state," said his friend Rich Clawson.

Frigo fell on the stairs on a Sunday and hung on till early Monday, when he died at Billings Clinic. He was 71.

Thousands of people who might not have known his name will probably remember Frigo the musician. He played the piano, organ, clarinet, trumpet, saxophone and trombone, and he was a good singer, too. He played at bars and other venues in Billings, Red Lodge and around the region, and most recently played piano at the Rex in downtown Billings on weekend nights.

He played jazz standards, show tunes, Dixieland, blues, country and pop. In the words of his friend Florence Stevens, herself a longtime pianist in Billings, "He knew just about every song. Boy, he knew music."

Norrine "The Outlaw Queen" Linderman, who played with Frigo hundreds of times around Montana and Wyoming, said Frigo was a musical genius, "one of the great musicians ever to hit Montana."

"I've had a lot of good bands in Montana, I tell you what, but Jimmie played with me more than anyone," she said.

His showstopper was pounding out a bass line on the piano with his left hand while playing trumpet with his right.

Like a lot of good musicians, Frigo also had a head for numbers. His oddest talent was telling you, instantly, what day of the week you were born on if you gave him the date and the year. Most people had to look it up themselves, and when they did, Frigo was invariably right.

In a similar vein, if he talked about something that happened to him in the past, he usually referenced the exact day, together with a description of that day's weather.

And once he knew your birthday or your wedding anniversary or any other important date, he never forgot it. Florence said Frigo used to play piano while her mother played harmonica. One day, years after her mother died, Florence found a photograph in her mailbox.

It was a beautiful picture of her mother's old house on the North Side, taken by Frigo. He also wrote a few lines about Florence's mother looking down from the sky. Florence had forgotten it was her mother's birthday, but Jim hadn't. That talent was part of what another friend, Christine Pierce, called Frigo's love for "the symbol of the days."

Frigo was famous for his love of cats. He always had at least a few of them living with him, and if he was down to his last dollar the cats would eat first. There was something obsessive about his love for cats, as if he tried to bring an order to the lives of animals that he couldn't bring to his own, but his tenderness toward them was something to see.

That tenderness extended to other creatures, too.

A friend, Margaret Cunningham, said Frigo "appreciated my

disinclination to kill spiders."

He rode an old 10-speed bicycle everywhere and sometimes his habitations were a little sketchy, but he always carried himself with dignity and he was always careful to repay a loan. He called on his many friends for help, but he also gave of his talents. For years he and Norrine played music at nursing homes and the Montana Rescue Mission, and Frigo volunteered his time to play piano in the cafeteria of St. Vincent Healthcare.

When it was time to perform, he always managed to make himself look good.

He'd put on a pair of black pants, a clean shirt and a vest, maybe wrap a bandana around his neck and don one of his hats, usually a Greek fisherman's cap or a fedora. With his gray goatee, and especially with his blue-tinted shades, he looked like an old hipster, and he played the part by sprinkling his speech with beatnikisms like "Yeah, man."

He was born on the South Side of Chicago and his mother, Eleanor, was a professional organist-pianist and teacher. Norrine said Frigo played the big hotels in Chicago and all over the Midwest before moving to Montana in 1986. He spent a couple of years in Miles City before settling in Billings. Other scraps of biographical information were shared around his deathbed.

Florence said Frigo had twin children, a boy and girl, still living in the Chicago area. Johnny Frigo, a famous jazz violinist who died a few years ago at 90, was said to be his cousin. Someone else said Frigo played clarinet with the Chicago Symphony in his younger days. Everyone had stories about Frigo's music, his wit, his facility with numbers, his cats.

On the way out, Frigo even managed to pay his own way. Clawson had recently helped Frigo obtain some long-overdue Social Security payments, and when he died he was carrying $968 in cash in his pants pocket. A funeral parlor agreed to accept that money for cremation and call it good.

"Isn't that the perfect ending?" Clawson said.

Originally published May 17, 2009, in The Billings Gazette

SHIRLEY SMITH:
COWBOY CURATOR

FROMBERG — Shirley Smith's establishment is called The Little Cowboy Bar and Museum, but you could think of it as a shrine.

It's a shrine to all the cowboys and cowgirls and rodeo riders that Smith has befriended over the years. And it's a shrine to Smith's corner of the world, the farm- and ranchland that stretches from the foothills of the Beartooths to the Pryor Mountains in the Clarks Fork River valley.

The low-slung bar on Fromberg's main drag has a green stucco front covered with red hand-painted brands, dozens of them from ranches around the valley. A weathered pair of silver-and-black cowboy boots has been converted to a set of planters, and an ancient saddle sits on a cross-bar over the hitching post. Inside is the long, narrow tavern that Smith bought in 1972. It is crowded with photographs of cowboys and bronc riders, and many of the photos bear autographs or inscriptions. Behind the barroom is the museum — a 20-foot-by-40-foot room Smith added on when her collection of memorabilia got too large.

The museum is packed with oddball curios, conversation pieces and artifacts of local history. There are beaded moccasins made by Crow, Cheyenne and Blackfeet Indians, badges, purses, belt buckles, a black parasol from the 1800s and a pistol that a 94-year-old sheepherder used to kill himself. There is a collection of clippings, documents and photographs about infamous local outlaw Earl Durand, branded "the Tarzan of the Tetons" by Eastern writers whose sense of drama exceeded their grasp of geography.

There are rifles and swords, a war club, old magazines and calendars, an antique vanity case, an original photograph of Buffalo Bill Cody and a complimentary pass to the 1910 edition of Cody's Wild West Show. Over in a corner, next to a large collection of mounted spiders, scorpions, beetles and bugs, gathered locally, there are two buffalo fetuses, a beaver fetus and a Jerusalem cricket, all preserved in alcohol.

But mostly, the museum is a celebration of rodeo cowboys, many of them from Montana and northern Wyoming. There is Turk Greenough's cowboy hat, Bud Linderman's bareback rigging, Bill Dygert's saddle, hat and bull rope, and an ornate leather cowboy hat once worn by Paul Holzum, a rodeo announcer in the 1930s and '40s. Other mementos, newspaper clippings, posters and photographs commemorate rodeo stars like Benny Binion, Rex Allen and Freckles Brown.

It was love that started Smith's infatuation with cowboys and the rodeo. She fell for a cowboy, Al Smith, and followed him from Wyoming to Montana in 1969. Shirley Smith eventually married Al, her second husband, who worked as a hand on the Greenough Ranch in the Sage Creek area of the Pryors. Through Al, Shirley Smith became good friends with most of the Greenoughs in the area, including Turk, Bill, Alice and Marge, all of whom are in the National Cowboy Hall of Fame in Oklahoma City.

A lot of that family tradition was distilled into Deb Greenough, a former world-champion rodeo cowboy who grew up in Fromberg and now lives outside Billings. Greenough remembers being a kid and winning a rodeo buckle for the first time. As soon as he got home, he ran down the street to the Little Cowboy Bar.

"Shirley was definitely one of 'em I couldn't wait to show," Greenough said.

A lot of other cowboys must have felt the same way. People were always bringing her collectibles and keepsakes, feeding a habit that Smith developed as a child. She spent her first seven years in a 10-foot-by-12-foot shed outside Byron, Wyo., with three siblings and her parents, though her father, a truck driver, sheep shearer and coal miner, was often away from home. Sometimes people from town would come out and dump their garbage near the family shack. The kids would hide until the people left, then pick through the trash in search of treasures.

"I'm a pack rat," Smith says. "I just love pretty things."

As her own collection of "pretty things" grew, cowboys, friends, customers, townfolk and tourists kept giving her memorabilia to add to her collection. Before she knew it, she wasn't just a bar owner but a collector, curator and director of her own museum.

Deb Greenough said he was always amazed at how much Smith collected and how well she displayed it.

"She's taken the past and preserved it," he said. "And that's pretty darned nice because I'd never have the patience to do it."

Shirley Smith is as much an attraction as her bar and museum. She still dresses like an old-time rodeo queen, what with her perfectly coiffed hair, a profusion of turquoise jewelry and a fringed leather vest. Under Smith's ownership, the Little Cowboy Bar has been one of the major gathering spots in Fromberg for more than 30 years.

"We've done everything in here but birthed a baby, and one day we got pretty close," she said. "We've set bones. I've pulled teeth. I've taken stitches out. I've taken ticks out of kids' ears. Lots of ticks."

Every Thanksgiving and Christmas, Smith makes turkey, ham and potatoes, and other people from the area bring in salads and side dishes. Then she lays the food out in the bar and invites all comers.

"Anybody that doesn't have anywhere to go — friend or foe — we feed 'em," she said. How many people usually show up? "Well," Smith said, "we don't have many leftovers."

She is so well-known in the valley that in the mid-1980s she served one term as mayor of Bridger. "They wrote me in," she said. "I think it's because my name was easy to spell."

Another honor came her way in 2001, when she was chosen as Ms. Senior Montana at a competition in Las Vegas. As for how old she is, that's none of your business.

"Age is a word, not a condition," she said. "I gave up aging a long time ago."

It must have worked, if you listen to Deb Greenough. "She always had the prettiest smile and the bubbliest face," he said. "She never seemed to age, that woman."

She has a no-nonsense outlook to accompany her pretty smile. Some of her patrons are pretty rough fellows, but her bar is generally peaceful.

"Most of 'em I've pretty well housebroke," she said. "No, I don't allow any fighting in there. I've got too much memorabilia."

One regular at the bar is Guy Sower, a retired farmer from the Edgar area.

"I don't know whether you call it farming or not," Sower said. "I raised hay and sheep, and I raised hell, I guess."

Until he retired, Sower said, "I never was much of a guy to go into bar." Now he likes to stop in once a day, mostly for the chance to visit.

There's lots of visiting to be done at the Little Cowboy and lots of stories to hear. Smith will tell you about the ghost of the bar's former owner, Hank Deines, who haunted the place until the day his wife died, years after his own death. She'll tell you about her encounters with famous actors and the visitors from all over the world who've signed her guestbook. Most of all, she'll tell you about the cowboys and rodeo people she's known.

"Every cowboy, every picture, we've got a story," she said. "Someday I'll put it in a book."

Originally published June 1, 2006, in The Billings Gazette

DAVE COLLINGS:
A LAW-AND-ORDER MAN

DEER LODGE — If you put people in a prison, whether it's in the middle of a city, the middle of a desert or an island in the middle of the ocean, some of the prisoners are going to try to get out. Montana's two state prisons have been in Powell County, the first one at the south end of Deer Lodge and the new one five miles west of town, at the base of the foothills of the Flint Creek Range.

For the past 11 years, every time an inmate has escaped from prison, he entered into the jurisdiction of Powell County Sheriff Dave Collings. In those 11 years, and in eight years as an under-sheriff, Collings has searched for escaped cons on foot, on horseback, by jeep, car, helicopter and airplane. He's scoured river banks, raked through fields and climbed mountains.

Some of the cons swim the Clark Fork River, others beeline for the railroad tracks, still others steal prison vehicles or arrange to be picked up by accomplices on the outside. The most inge-nious escape Collings remembers involved a man who contrived to have himself trucked out of prison by hiding in a big box that was used by the prison bakery to deliver bread.

In the old days, not many of the hard-core prisoners escaped from behind the thick stone walls of the original prison in Deer Lodge. Most of the escapees were low-risk, minimum-security inmates from the prison ranch or from what was called Rothe Hall. That was a separate facility for prisoners who worked on the ranch or were coming up soon for parole. Collings remembers when 12 prisoners — the "dirty dozen," they were called — escaped en masse from Rothe Hall. None of them was considered dangerous, but Collings recalled with a sigh how long it took to round them all up.

A good many of the people who escape nowadays are dangerous, and when Collings is out at night looking for them, knowing they may be armed, "the apprehension of death is there. You make a foolish mistake and you're going to pay the penalty." Still, as he says, "That's your job. Let's just put it that way. You have to do something."

One thing that makes him feel safer is that he usually searches in the company of his dog, an English breed that resembles a Doberman.

"She's not trained to search or anything, but she can be vicious. There's no doubt in my mind that she'd tear hell out of somebody who tried to grab me." But even with all the searches Collings has been on, "I can't say I've ever really been threatened. I've never been shot at."

For his part, Collings has never shot at an escapee. When three escaped cons took three hostages in mid-October, however, it was Collings who decided to shoot their stolen escape vehicle to a halt. It worked. The tires were shot out, the car stopped, the hostages were freed, two inmates were captured and no one was hurt. As a result of that escape and because hostages were taken, a group of Deer Lodge Valley residents recently revived the Citizens Protective Association, designed to focus attention on security problems at the prison and to safeguard residents in the event of an escape. Collings thinks the best security measure would be to build a new, separate facility, similar to the old Rothe Hall, to house strictly low-security inmates.

No matter how tight the security, there will always be escapes, and as long as Collings is sheriff, he will have to respond. Fortunately, not all the encounters with escapees are as hair-raising as the October encounter with the speeding car full of cons.

One time, when he was with another searcher, "we had two guys swim the river on us. Me and the other guy flipped a coin to see who had to go after them. ... I happened to win." While his partner crossed the river, Collings checked the near bank, looking for the escapees. It wasn't long before he found one of them lying in a shallow, muddy spot with his head underwater and grass heaped up on his chest. The ex-jailbird was breathing through a bulrush. "All I could see was his nose and his red hair," Collings said.

Another time, Collings drove to Drummond after getting a tip that an escapee was there. Collings was dressed in worn, dirty clothes and did not look terribly official at the time.

"I just leaned up against the hotel and he just walked up and started talking to me. I told him he was under arrest."

Originally published November 7, 1981, in The Montana Standard

MONTANA BAR:
MARKING TIME IN MILES CITY

MILES CITY — Chris Cameron has been a regular at the Montana Bar for years, and no wonder.

The place is rich in history, for the people of Miles City and for Cameron's family in particular. When Cameron's father emigrated from Scotland in 1910, he made his way from Ellis Island to Terry, Mont.

The folks in Terry sent him along to Miles City. They told him to find the Montana Bar — look for the joint with the big stuffed sheep in the front window — and the people there would see that he found a job as a sheepherder.

"There was an awful lot of Scotsmen that came to this part of the country at that time," Cameron said.

Cameron remembers going to the Montana Bar as a young boy, where he would sit in the front booth, partitioned off from the rest of the bar, reserved for children. Years later, one of his jobs was to drive to town at the end of the weekend to pick up the sheepherders from his father's ranch. After a couple of rowdy days in Miles City, they would be waiting for him at the Montana Bar, tired, hung over and probably broke.

James Kenney ran a saddlery on Main Street from 1900 to

1907. He opened the Montana Bar in the saddlery building in 1908.

All these years later, the Montana Bar looks much as it did during its glory days. There is the three-arch back bar, matching liquor hutch and an icebox converted to a walk-in cooler, all of them made of oak. The original paddle fans still hang from the pressed-tin ceiling, and the floor is covered with Italian terrazzo tile, little hexagons of blue, gold, green, white and plum.

Big, dark booths and cherry-wood tables line the east wall of the bar, and the mounted heads of six longhorn steers and one small bison look down from just below the ceiling. In the front entryway are oak partition panels with beveled glass.

Miles City is Montana's pre-eminent cow town (OK, cow and sheep town), and the Montana Bar is most likely the best-preserved Old West bar in the state.

Joan Melcher, daughter of former U.S. Sen. John Melcher, wrote the book on Montana taverns in 1980. In "Watering Hole: A User's Guide to Montana Bars," Melcher set out to find the perfect tavern. The Montana Bar, she concluded, was probably "about as close to perfect as I was going to find."

A National Register of Historic Places plaque in the front window of the Montana says it "has been proclaimed by connoisseurs the perfect bar." Melcher, reached recently in Missoula, said she didn't know if she was one of the connoisseurs referred to, but she stands by her earlier judgment.

"I don't think I found one any better in terms of physical attributes," she said.

Amorette Allison, the historic preservation officer for Miles City, concurs. There may be bars in Montana that are older or that have some features as distinctive as the Montana, but she knows of no others that have remained virtually the same for so long.

"Even when they did do some remodeling, they didn't do anything drastic," she said. "It looked the same for years and years and years."

It's also a hit with people in the history business.

"Every time somebody comes down from the state Historical Society, we have to make a pilgrimage to the Montana Bar, and sometimes into the men's room," she said.

Yes, even the men's room. With its marble-walled stall and stout wooden door, tile floor and double-berth marble urinal, it's worth a look.

Looking at the preserved splendor of the Montana Bar, it's hard to believe it was almost demolished 20 years ago.

In 1985, an old hotel attached to the western wall of the Montana Bar burned down. Though the interior of the bar didn't suffer much damage, the fire burned six inches off the joists on the second floor of the building, seriously compromising the structural integrity of the west wall. The bar was closed for nearly four years, and the building was condemned, with orange stickers affixed to the front windows saying it was scheduled for demolition.

Enter Terry Hanson, a Miles City lawyer who said he had known the Montana for most of his life, starting when he used to hawk newspapers there as a second-grader. He had a client from Minnesota who was interested in buying the bar, so Hanson formed a corporation and entered into an agreement to buy the historic property. At the last moment, the Minnesotan backed out of the deal.

Hanson, a big, flamboyant man given to large gestures, decided to go into the bar business.

"I had just hit a good lick on a lawsuit, so I had some cash," he said.

His wife, Deborah, was in the travel business and was on a month-long tour of China when the deal on the Montana went down.

"When she came back, she said, 'What's new?' I said, 'Well, I just bought a bar.' "

The Hansons formed a corporation, Watering Hole Inc., with three other couples and four individuals dedicated to preserving the historic bar. At the time, Hanson said, "it was pretty much a mess."

The three-arch back bar was in the garage. The booths, still upholstered in their original horsehair, were stored in the basement, as were the tables, the beveled-glass panels and the liquor hutch, which was in several pieces.

Fortunately, the building and all the furnishings were so well made and had suffered so little damage over the years that they mostly just needed a good cleaning. That's why the renovation, which looks as though it must have been expensive, cost only $70,000 — that and a lot of time and effort.

"I was the general contractor," Hanson said. "I didn't get much legal work done that year."

Before he reopened the bar in 1989, Hanson also reclaimed the stuffed Audubon's sheep that stood in the front window for so many years. He knew it had been donated to the local Fish and Game office, which had hopes of putting the sheep, a member of a now-extinct species, in a museum. Hanson convinced them that the sheep belonged back at the Montana.

"It's in a museum now," Hanson said. "A functional museum."

The extensive woodwork was restored by two local craftsmen, Dominique Pinoteau and Raymond Muggli, whose efforts are commemorated on a small brass plaque attached to the bar. Hanson relied on his memories of the old Montana Bar to place the oak partitions in the same positions they occupied years ago. A red longhorn steer and the diminutive bison were the only mounts in the original bar. Hanson acquired the new animals, including one from a bar in Wibaux and another from a bar in Winnett.

During the five years Hanson and the Watering Hole investors owned the Montana, Deborah Hanson was the manager, working behind the bar. She had the floors polished once a week and ran a no-nonsense establishment, allowing no fighting or undue rowdiness. Once, Terry Hanson admitted, he got into a bit of a spat with another patron and his wife kicked both of them out of the bar.

In 1994, Hanson and his partners sold the Montana Bar to another Miles City corporation, Lone Buckaroo Inc. Currie Colvin and John Leitholt currently manage the Montana for the corporation, and they are credited by Hanson and others with keeping the Montana in prime condition.

Leitholt said a combination of good stewardship and sound construction helps keep the bar in good shape, even during crowded, raucous events like the annual Bucking Horse Sale.

"It's pretty sturdy stuff," Leitholt said, looking around the bar.

Last year, Lone Buckaroo bought the empty storefront on the east side of the Montana Bar. The corporation has since restored the space and rents it out for weddings, birthday parties and other events.

Colvin hopes to name it the Charlie Brown Room in honor of a Miles City pioneer who opened one of the first bars in town. Colvin said Brown used to let cowboys sleep on the floor and buy them their first shot in the morning. By coincidence, Hanson once found, in the basement of his old house just off Main Street, a photograph of Charlie Brown taken by famous early-day photographer L.A. Huffman.

It's that sense of connection with history that inspired Hanson and his partners to buy the Montana Bar, and which animates the current group of owners.

"Nobody really owns it," Colvin said. "We just manage it, like the fair board or something."

Originally published January 31, 2007, in The Billings Gazette

ELIZABETH BAKER:
A SELF-SUSTAINING WOMAN

BILLINGS — Five months ago, at the age of 94, Elizabeth Baker moved into a nursing home. For the first time in 38 years, she had running water and electricity. She had heat that didn't involve shoveling coal or stuffing wood into a stove. And she had plenty of company after years of voluntary seclusion.

For Elizabeth, solitude was a small patch of land and a 24-by-8-foot shack on the bluffs overlooking the Yellowstone River on the site of an old gravel pit.

She canned food, hauled her own water, collected edible and medicinal plants, carefully stretched out her meager income and walked just about everywhere she needed to go. She doesn't mind talking about her life, but she delivers a warning first.

"It isn't going to be a happy story," she says. "It's a story of despair and sorrow and suffering."

That's what she says. But as her story spills out, delivered in a rapid monotone and embroidered with details that someone her age could be forgiven for having forgotten, she looks anything but sad. She glows with pride at having lived a life of her own choosing, and her old eyes flash with sparks of independence.

Before settling above the river, Elizabeth lived a life of hard knocks. She was born in northern Idaho in 1908, then moved to Montana after her father's death. She was married at 20, widowed at 31. She helped raise five girls — her daughter and four daughters of a man who'd lost his wife.

Eventually, she moved to Billings, where she studied accounting. That's also where she made what she calls her big mistake: she went too far while praying for help in completing her studies.

"I told Him if He'd help me I'd never ask His help again," she says. "The Bible says, swear not by anything. I didn't swear, but I tried to make a contract with God, I guess."

Things never quite worked out for her after that. She was a good accountant, she says, but she wasn't able to hold a job long. She says people picked on her because of medical problems related to her premature birth.

"People who couldn't see my disability called me lazy," she says.

But she was determined to make it on her own. That's how she ended up in a shack above the river.

After her daughter grew up, Elizabeth lived with her for a time in Butte, but not wanting to be a burden, she moved back to Billings. She had been collecting Social Security since her husband died, and though it wasn't much, she managed to live on that and whatever she raised through odd jobs, or even looking for change on the streets.

"I did everything I could to get me a penny, as long as it was honest and legal," she says. "I never stole anything in my life."

She says she sometimes slept in brush by the river and once slept under farm machinery on a sales lot in the Heights. Then, in 1964, she found a permanent home. A friend sold her an oil field construction shack, complete with a stove, for $1. She lived in it for four years on North 13th Street before having it moved to what used to be a gravel pit above Two Moon Park.

An acquaintance moved it for her. "He said if I wanted to stay off welfare, he'd move it free." Elizabeth says she got legal advice to the effect that she could legally squat on the county-owned land.

However it came about, that's where she lived until last fall, in a secluded swale surrounded by trees, with views up and down the river. Elizabeth built three small outbuildings on the property, crudely constructed of scrap wood, tar paper and odd sheets of corrugated steel. She decorated the buildings with horseshoes, faucet handles, chains, gears and small spoked wheels, some of which she painted. On one side of the property is a hand-dug privy.

Everywhere there is evidence of a whimsical ingenuity, as if Robinson Crusoe had been shipwrecked on the shores of the Yellowstone.

On top of a heap of rusty stovepipes is Elizabeth's old green cart, the one she used for so many years to bring home water, groceries and other supplies. Elizabeth walked everywhere, and one thing she splurged on was good footwear — Red Wing men's work boots.

She learned much about gathering plants as a child, and she taught herself more as an adult. She ate dandelion salads and she swears by dock, a common plant loaded with iron and vitamins C and A. She gathered chokecherries and currants, and neighbors would bring her heaps of windfall apples.

Thanks to her frugality and her very limited needs, she managed to save money, and twice a year she'd give $15 to the Montana Rescue Mission. As she puts it, "I used to send some money to my fellow man."

She was befriended by many people over the years, but only rarely did she consent to accept their charity. She'd take a ride now and then, and in recent years she allowed people to help her chop wood, to bring her jugs of water or to buy her a little food.

Rita Starr, who lives on Bench Boulevard not far from Centennial Arena, used to see Elizabeth on her wanderings. She became her friend after stopping one day to strike up a conversation. Rita said a dozen or more people regularly checked up on Elizabeth or helped her out one way or another, but mostly Elizabeth just wanted to be alone, with only a dog or a cat or two for company. She loved to spend hours sitting under the trees looking out over the river, daydreaming, napping or reading her Bible.

She made her own candles out of paraffin, using the seam from blue jeans for a wick, and that was her only light. Coal was delivered once a year from Roundup, in big chunks that she'd have to break up into pieces small enough for her stove. Wood scraps supplemented the coal.

For many years she had no refrigeration at all, until Rita gave her a cooler and started supplying her with milk jugs full of ice. Elizabeth paid taxes on her property — $63.75 last year — kept scrapbooks, went for walks, collected plants and listened to National Public Radio on her transistor radio. She often surprised people with her knowledge of current events.

She says she was bitten by a rattlesnake once years ago, but she didn't seek medical help. She just waited it out, resting up all one summer until the pain went away.

She was determined not to give up her independence, until last fall. In mid-November, bending over to pick something up, she slipped and fell, breaking her collarbone and hitting her head on the stove. She lay there for two hours before dragging herself into bed.

Rita happened to stop by the next day, and as she walked up to the gate, Elizabeth, still in pain, approached her and said, "You're just the person I wanted to see. I can no longer take care of myself."

On Nov. 15, Elizabeth moved into Eagle Cliff Manor, a nursing home on Yellowstone River Road, not far from the downstream end of Two Moon Park. Rita thought Elizabeth might not take to the nursing home after so many years alone, but she seems to be doing fine, and she admits to needing help.

"The shack's wore out and so am I," she says.

She used her savings to buy some new clothes, a pair of glasses and dentures, replacing a set that was 60 years old. She also bought a battery-powered radio with a hand crank for use in emergencies.

She wants to be ready for whatever might happen.

Originally published April 27, 2003, in The Billings Gazette

WARREN JONES:
THE NIGHT THE OLYMPIAN WRECKED

BILLINGS — Warren Jones and Maurice Odquist were among the passengers on the Milwaukee railroad's Olympian train just after midnight on June 19, 1938, when the train plunged into the rain-swollen waters of Custer Creek, 26 miles east of Miles City.

Nearly 50 people were killed and scores more were injured, but Jones and Odquist were unhurt. As it happened, they were both packing cameras, and as soon as it was light enough, they began photographing the dramatic, devastating scene, the worst train wreck in the history of Montana. They ended up shooting remarkably similar pictures of twisted wreckage and partly submerged passenger cars.

Jones sent his film to his father in Milwaukee to have it developed. Odquist apparently sent his to Life magazine as quickly as he could. On July 4, 1938, Life splashed Odquist's photos all over a spread that was headlined "A Survivor Photographs the Worst American Train Wreck Since 1887."

"He was the smart one," said Jones, a rancher and banker who spent most of his life in Harlowton and now lives in Billings.

Not that Jones was looking for glory, then or now.

"I've always said, we were more spectators than survivors."

Jones was born in Butte and his family moved to Milwaukee when he was 7 or 8, but he used to return to Montana every summer to spend time on his mother's family's ranch near Two Dot. In 1938, when Jones was 17, he and his cousin, John Baxter, who was 10 or 11, booked passage out to Montana aboard the Olympian.

The Olympian, as every Milwaukee train that ran between Chicago and Tacoma was known, was a fast, air-conditioned train, described in a contemporary newspaper account as "the railroad's pride." Shortly before their departure, Jones' father changed the boys' accommodations, moving them from a "tourist" Pullman car into a standard Pullman, which was roomier. That decision probably saved their lives.

Jones and his cousin boarded the train in Milwaukee, chugging into Montana about 10 p.m. on June 18. They crossed the Yellowstone River at the Calypso bridge near Terry, next stop Miles City, passing through country that Jones said was "about as deserted a chunk of Montana as you can find." Jones was sleeping in a lower berth, with his cousin up above. It was quiet, thanks to the heavy green curtains sealing off each berth.

At 12:35 a.m., the train came to a shuddering halt. Back in his sleeper car, a car or two away from the observation car that brought up the rear of the 11-car train, Jones wasn't even aware that the train had wrecked.

"I didn't have any sense of being in an impact accident," he said. "I just became aware of that fact that it had gotten awfully quiet." Though he heard little and saw nothing, Jones has vivid memories of a particular odor.

"The thing I remember more clearly than anything else was becoming aware, as I woke up, of the overpowering odor of sage brush," he said.

It was the smell of all the sage that had been ripped from the hills and plains in the Custer Creek drainage, which had just been hit with what The Billings Gazette would refer to the next day as a "cloudburst of unprecedented proportions." Twenty minutes before the disaster, a Milwaukee station agent reported that Custer Creek was carrying about 4 feet of water. That was a lot for the usually dry creek, but nothing to worry about.

Then came the flash flood. By the time the Olympian reached Custer Creek, the stream was flowing at an estimated depth of 20 feet, creating enough force to weaken the two middle piers of the iron and concrete trestle, which was 180 feet long. When the train passed over the first weakened support, it gave way. The engine and its tender car flew through the air into the west bank of the creek. The mail and baggage cars smashed into the engine, with two day coaches and one of the tourist sleepers just behind them.

It was determined later, when the speed-recorder tape on the locomotive was recovered, that the Olympian was traveling at 51 mph, well under the speed limit of 65 for that stretch of track. Still, 51 mph makes for a great deal of momentum, given that the engine and its tender together weighed 440 tons. The wreck left the two other tourist sleepers in the middle of the creek, rapidly filling with water and silt. Jones' Pullman was high and dry on the undamaged tracks on the east side of Custer Creek, and inside the sleeper everything was strangely calm.

"There was no running up and down the aisle screaming and crying," Jones said. "It was really rather quiet. The only problem I remember, some people were having trouble finding their shoes because they'd set them down and they slid down the aisle."

Jones said his cousin didn't even wake up, so he roused him.

"I said, 'John, I think we're in a wreck, and we're probably going to be late into Harlo in the morning.' And he says, 'Shit,' and went back to sleep."

A brakeman got out of the train to walk back to put some flares behind the train, but Jones doesn't remember anyone else going outside. There was nothing they could do anyway, since everyone who needed help was in the raging creek or on the other side of the washed-out bridge. And if you looked out the window, all you could see in the dark was water everywhere, seemingly on all sides.

Jones made his way through his car and into the dining car, where he met a porter and a dining room conductor. They had just crawled out of one of the tourist Pullmans, ahead of the dining car. It was still attached to the diner, but teetering precariously over the water, into which it soon fell.

"They didn't say much at all," Jones recalled. "They were

both in a state of excitement and shock."

After a while, Jones went back to sleep. At first light, a few passengers started wandering outside. Among them were Jones and Odquist, both with their cameras. Jones was carrying his Contax, a German-made camera that used 35mm film. Shortly after he went outside, Jones said, a rescue engine from Miles City pulled up on the other side of Custer Creek. It had come out of the west, and its headlight stood out against the dark sky behind it.

Jones snapped a picture just as the engine's headlight appeared over the top of the crippled locomotive that had been pulling the Olympian. A virtually identical photo, though with a man standing on top of one of the downed railroad cars, was taken by Odquist and was the photo featured on the first page of the Life magazine spread.

It was described as being the first picture of the wreck, but Jones doesn't think so. The sky is noticeably darker in his photo, Jones said, and the train cars in the foreground are almost black, whereas in Odquist's photo quite a bit of detail is visible on the cars. It is possible to lighten some photos in the darkroom, but Jones said his photo was taken when it was so dark that no amount of work in the darkroom would have brought up any additional details of the cars in the foreground.

Jones said he and Odquist shot some other pictures from the same perspective. He even remembers bumping into Odquist while getting one photo, though at the time he didn't know who he was. Jones doesn't recall hearing anything but the sound of rushing water.

After he shot the last 12 frames on his roll of film, Jones went back to his car, which eventually was taken by another engine to the Northern Pacific tracks south of the river, and then on to Miles City, which they reached about 3:30 on the afternoon of June 19. From there, after letting their families know they were safe, Jones and his cousin continued on to the station in Harlowton, and then to the ranch near Two Dot.

At the ranch, Jones mailed his film back to his father in Milwaukee. His father, also a photo buff, used to develop all of his son's film. Jones never did see the negatives. His father sent him back 5-by-7-inch prints of the wreck. Jones said Odquist, described by Life as head of the marketing division for the American Can Co., had been traveling by train from Florida to Seattle.

Meanwhile, recovery efforts at Custer Creek continued for days. The official count of the dead at the time was 47, with 60 others injured. The body of a woman believed to have been a passenger on the train was found in the Yellowstone River the next day at Glendive, 50 miles away. Custer Creek dumped into the Yellowstone 2,500 feet south of the railroad bridge.

Another body was found in the river at Sidney three months after the wreck. The Gazette reported that one recovered body was determined to have been an embalmed corpse that was being carried on the train.

Originally published April 11, 2006, in The Billings Gazette

MYRTLE HOFACKER:
LOVE AND WAR

BILLINGS — Myrtle Hofacker was married in Paris in the month of June, in a candlelight ceremony in a chapel decorated with sweet peas and white gladioluses. It doesn't get much more romantic than that.

But she and her husband had earned it, for theirs was a wartime courtship that began in Iceland and continued in England and France, stretching out over nearly three years.

Myrtle was 25 when she joined the Army as a nurse in the spring of 1942. She was a small-town girl from Ohio, one of six children, and she was already a registered nurse when she enlisted as a second lieutenant. When the Army asked for volunteers for overseas duty, Myrtle stepped forward again. She and other nurses shipped out for Iceland in August, though they didn't know their destination when they embarked.

"We never thought that we'd be gone from our families and our country for three years," she said.

The ship was part of a large convoy that came under German submarine attack a few hundred miles from Iceland. At one point there was a "terrific explosion," so loud that people on Myrtle's ship thought it had been hit. It was actually a tanker running alongside their ship that was sunk by a torpedo.

Myrtle knew nothing of Iceland at the time.

"I barely knew it existed," she said. "I don't think any of us did."

The 50,000 American troops stationed on the island nation certainly knew about the contingent of American nurses.

"There were only 100 nurses, so we were quite popular. We were invited to all the officers' clubs," Myrtle said.

One night, about three weeks after her arrival in Iceland, Myrtle was invited to the officers' club of the 50th Signal Battalion. She spent most of the night dancing, and toward the end of the evening someone offered to buy her a drink. She said she didn't drink.

As Myrtle tells it, "The officer on my left said, 'We have some Coke if you prefer that.'"

That offer of a Coke was all it took.

"I just liked him from the moment we met," Myrtle said. "And I guess he shared the same feeling."

The young officer was Roger Hofacker, a native of Bismarck, N.D., who had grown up in Billings and graduated from Billings High School in 1933. An electrical engineer, he worked for Montana Power Co. for a couple of years before enlisting in the Army. He was called to active duty in the Army Signal Corps in 1941.

During their 14 months in Iceland, Myrtle and Roger went to movies together, watched the Northern Lights dancing over Reykjavik or just sat talking in the lounge of the nurses' quarters.

Iceland was an important stop on the shipping lanes that carried American-made armaments and other goods to the Russians. German observation planes sometimes flew over Iceland, but there was no bombing, so where Myrtle and the other nurses worked was basically like a hospital for a city of 50,000, except that the population consisted entirely of young men.

Myrtle and Roger embarked for England, on separate ships, on Nov. 1, 1943. The trip to Iceland had been on calm seas, but during the four-day voyage to England the convoy ran into a North Atlantic storm. The nurses were stacked three bunks high in small compartments, and everyone was violently ill.

They disembarked in northern Scotland, greeted by a bagpipe band, then traveled by train to their posts in England. Myrtle went to a hospital in Blockley, west of London, where she and five other nurses shared a small Quonset hut. It was common knowledge that the Allies were preparing for an invasion of the European continent.

"Every roadway was lined with supplies, and Americans were everywhere," Myrtle said.

She had been exchanging letters — almost every day — with Roger, who was stationed near Salisbury, about 80 miles south of Blockley. Roger managed to get a leave and visit Myrtle in Blockley on New Year's Eve. It was the first time they had seen each other since Iceland, and they danced until midnight.

"Then we went back to the nurses' lounge and we got engaged," she said.

They had a five-day leave together in Scotland in February, and Roger saw Myrtle one more time in England, in May. By then, he was sure he would soon be joining the invasion of Europe.

"It was a year before I saw him again," Myrtle said.

On the night of June 5-6, 1944, masses of planes were flying overhead all night long, so Myrtle and the other nurses knew the invasion was under way before it was formally announced on June 6. Roger went ashore in Normandy on Day 2.

Back in England, Myrtle was working the night shift in the operating room of the hospital in Blockley. The wounded from the D-Day landing started coming in the first day, June 6, and the OR stayed busy 24 hours a day for the next several weeks. By then, the Allies had advanced far enough to set up hospitals in France, taking some of the pressure off Myrtle's hospital.

In November, her hospital began taking in German prisoners of war. "That was different, but it was the same type of injuries," she said.

She remembers hearing the German soldiers singing familiar Christmas songs but in their own language, and they were so accustomed to military discipline that when she, a lieutenant, walked onto the ward, all those who could stand sprang to attention. The rest fell silent until she gave the "at ease" command.

It was a sad Christmas for Myrtle. It was her third holiday overseas, and her younger brother, a 19-year-old Marine named

Lloyd, had been killed that year in the Pacific, in the battle for the island of Guam. Another brother, Elmer, was serving in Europe and would survive the war.

In January 1944, German doctors and corpsmen took over the medical care at the POW hospital in Blockley, and Myrtle and the other nurses were sent to France. After serving for a short time at a hospital in Le Havre, Myrtle was dispatched to Paris, where she arrived on the first day of spring.

In Paris, she worked in a hospital's neurological unit, treating soldiers with head and spinal injuries.

"It was so sad," she said. "It was just one ward in one hospital, so you knew how many thousands there were in the same condition."

She hadn't seen Roger since just before D-Day, but they had continued to exchange letters. One day in mid-May, not long after victory had been declared in Europe, Myrtle was told she had a visitor. It was Roger, back from leave. He thought he could get back to Paris again on June 10 and suggested that they get married that day. Myrtle was all for it, but June 10 came and went and Roger didn't show.

He finally arrived on the 14th. Myrtle had to work the next morning at 7, but she managed to obtain leave that afternoon. French law required Roger and Myrtle to exchange vows in a French civil ceremony, so the head nurse at Myrtle's hospital got them a car and driver and whisked them to a district courthouse in Paris.

"We had an interpreter," Myrtle said. "He said the only thing we had to say was 'Oui.' "

They went straight from the courthouse to the hospital chapel, where they were wed by an American chaplain, in what Myrtle's hometown paper described as "an impressive candlelight ceremony." The head nurse played the piano, and Myrtle's good friend and fellow nurse, Hila Clevenger, was her attendant.

"It was kind of a rushed affair, but it worked," Myrtle said.

Their honeymoon was a week in Paris. They stayed in a special Army hotel for married couples and received free meals and transportation, also courtesy of the Army.

"Our whole honeymoon cost us the champagne we had in the nightclub," Myrtle said.

They would soon return to the United States, Myrtle in August 1945 and Roger in October. Roger went back to work for Montana Power Co., and the couple lived in Helena, Lewistown, Livingston, Butte and Colstrip before he retired as a senior vice president in 1980.

They traveled extensively after Roger's retirement, eventually visiting every continent, including Antarctica. They made one trip back to Iceland, for their 55th wedding anniversary in 2000, and they visited England and France many times over the years.

They moved to Whitefish after Roger retired and lived there until September 2003, when they moved to Billings to be closer to one of their sons. Roger died a short time later, in October 2003. Myrtle, who turns 91 next month, lives in the Heights, not far from her son's family.

Looking back on her three years' service during World War II, she speaks with a matter-of-fact pride.

Myrtle said she "almost felt privileged" to have been part of the war effort, and she doesn't remember the decision to enlist being very difficult.

"I wasn't married and didn't have any children," she said. "People were very patriotic at that time, and it was just the right thing to do."

Originally published September 1, 2007, in The Billings Gazette

WARREN McGEE:
TRAIN HISTORIAN

LIVINGSTON — Sitting in Martin's Café, in what used to be the old beanery attached to the Northern Pacific Railway depot, Warren McGee motions out the window with his thumb.

"I've been running up and down that platform since I was 4 years old," he says.

That was 87 years ago. As a boy, he could identify almost all the locomotives that rolled into the Livingston yards just by hearing their bells and whistles. A lot of times, he could even tell you who the engineer was before he saw the train.

Like his father and his mother's father before him, McGee went on to work for the railroad, first as a brakeman and then a conductor, in a career that lasted 35 years. The work didn't dampen his enthusiasm. His boyhood fascination with trains, and with locomotives in particular, only grew.

His love for the old locomotives may have had something to do with professional pride, but he was also a photographer, and what photographer could resist their innumerable cogs, gears, levers and wheels, not to mention their billowing clouds of steam, the very emblems of power and speed?

For more than 60 years, on the job and in his free time,

McGee took photographs of trains — so many that he donated nearly 48,000 negatives, slides and prints to the Montana Historical Society. He still has 3,000 to 4,000 more at home, and those will eventually go to Helena, too.

Though the Northern Pacific is his specialty, McGee's interests are wide, and his passion for research and collecting is bottomless. In addition to photographs, he has donated 19 boxes of manuscripts, letters, books and documents to the historical society. In the basement of the house he has lived in for 51 years, hundreds more loose-leaf binders are stuffed with information on dozens of subjects, including alternative energy, Montana historical sites, taxes, politics, World War II, dams, oil and gas, riverboats and mining.

He was just as meticulous in organizing his photographs, making sure that each carried a record of where it was taken, what the engine number was, who was in the picture and everything else McGee deemed important. As he says in his railroad man's gruff but somehow inoffensive way, "I tried to tell 'em why I took the damn picture."

All that is for posterity. In the meantime, McGee seems to have every one of those facts filed away in his 91-year-old head. He reels off dates, distances, weights, names, numbers and addresses as if he's reading from a book.

Rufus Cone, a physics professor at Montana State University in Bozeman, a train buff and a friend of McGee's for many years, related an instance of McGee's amazing recall. An acquaintance who was about to publish a photograph of a train chugging along the Jefferson River once asked Cone for help nailing down where the photo was taken. Cone couldn't tell, so he asked McGee, who had traveled that route countless times.

McGee took one look at the photo and gave the location — at such and such a point between two mileposts. Later research showed that his snap pronouncement was accurate within a tenth of a mile.

"It's just mind-boggling," Cone said.

McGee's maternal grandfather was a conductor on the famous Rock Island Line in Illinois before he came out to Livingston to work for the Northern Pacific in 1890. McGee's father, Howard, moved to Livingston in 1907 and worked for the railroad for more than 50 years, three years as a fireman and 49 as an engineer.

The firemen shoveled coal from the tender car into the steam engine on the locomotive. McGee offers a more evocative description of the job: "Head down, tail up." He also has a short way of explaining the difference between an engineer and a conductor: "The engineer's running the engine; the conductor's running the train."

McGee couldn't wait to follow the footsteps of his father and grandfather, but when he graduated from high school in 1933, work on the railroad was scarce. Instead, he signed on as a dishwasher in the kitchen serving crews on one of the biggest construction projects in Montana history — the Cooke City Highway.

Even back then, he packed a camera wherever he went. His older brother, who went on to become a professional photographer, had gotten interested in cameras first, and McGee bought his first one, an Agfa Readyset, as a teenager. After working all day washing dishes, he'd hike up switchbacks to get photos of the slowly growing alpine road.

"I had the first pictures of that goddamned highway and didn't know it," he said.

He held down a few other jobs before finally going to work with the railroad on July 11, 1936, starting out as a brakeman. His career was interrupted six years later, when he was drafted by the Army. McGee declined Uncle Sam's assignment to do aerial photography in the Army Air Corps.

"I saw how they flew those airplanes and said no goddamned way."

Instead, he worked as a photo lab maintenance man and airplane mechanic, serving at Guadalcanal, Bougainville and the Marianas, among other locations in the Pacific. While he was at war on the other side of the world, he retained his seniority back home and was automatically promoted to conductor, the post he took up when he was discharged in September 1945.

Eager as he was to get back to Livingston, McGee made stops in Seattle, Tacoma and Spokane so he could get photographs of some Northern Pacific locomotives he hadn't added to his collection. For the rest of his 29-year stint as a conductor,

McGee was rarely without a camera. He had many over the years, but his favorite was an Eastman Kodak 616 Special, a relatively compact camera he packed under his left armpit, "just like a pistol."

He calls that camera "my pet" because it was small and easy to use. He generally preset the shutter speed at 1/200th of a second, with an F-stop of 11, which was just right for the outdoor shooting he was accustomed to. He got a lot of photographs in the various yards and in the big roundhouse shops in Bozeman, but mostly he liked to shoot trains rolling down the line.

In the words of Gary Tarbox, president of the Northern Pacific Railway Historical Association, "There's always a lot of Montana in his photos." Tarbox, a retired Microsoft employee who lives in Seattle, went out with McGee on a shoot a couple of years ago, just to see the old master in action.

Tarbox said McGee told him, "The way you take a picture is, you find a pretty spot and let the train come through it."

Of course, it wasn't that easy. McGee was familiar with every inch of Northern Pacific line between Butte and Billings, and lots of other track as well, so he knew where the good photos were. But getting to the right spot at the right time of day, when the right train was coming down the track — that could be difficult.

"It takes sometimes 15 or 20 years to get the picture," McGee says. It's even more difficult now because McGee is nearly blind, with only limited peripheral vision. But he can still preset the functions on his camera and take a decent photograph.

His favorite stretch for photos was about 15 miles east of Livingston. There are hills you can climb to get a good perspective, and for a backdrop there is the Yellowstone River, rolling hills and rocky bluffs.

"You've got to put something behind that train besides a damn boxcar," McGee said.

Sometimes he'd drive to a likely spot on his days off, but mostly he snapped his photos on the job. If the train he was riding on had to pull off at a siding to let a faster train go through, he'd jump off and start hoofing it up hills and over fences, getting in position before the passing train came his way. If he knew he couldn't make it back by the time his train left, he'd arrange to have the engineer slow down so he could hop aboard as the train passed him.

He liked to photograph trains on a big S-curve, which showed a lot of the cars, and like all the old railroad photographers he loved the steam engines.

"You can't beat smoke for showing action," he said.

But whether it was steam or diesel, in motion or in the yard, McGee's overriding aim was to get a photo of every locomotive on the Northern Pacific. He came up a little short, he said, but it wasn't for lack of trying. At least once a year he'd go to the yards in Seattle or St. Paul, Minn., to bag another locomotive, or he'd find a photographer who had a picture of a missing locomotive. He'd then get permission to shoot a copy of the print. The only time he ever used a tripod, he said, was in shooting those copies.

By the early 1990s, McGee realized his photographs needed to go someplace safe. Working with Cone, the physics professor at Bozeman, McGee started donating his work to the Montana Historical Society about five years ago. He kept adding to the stream of photos, prints and negatives as he finished cataloging them, and the Northern Pacific Railway Historical Association gave the historical society $15,000 to process and conserve the photographs.

Lori Morrow, photograph archives supervisor for the historical society, said there are other prominent photographers whose railroad-related works have made their way into the society's collection, but in terms of volume, record-keeping and sense of purpose, McGee's work "pretty much stands out alone."

He was able to keep that focus because of his fierce devotion to the Northern Pacific and to Livingston, the town the Northern Pacific built. In the decade leading up to the merger that swallowed the Northern Pacific and created the Burlington Northern Railroad in 1970, McGee was a leader of the fight to stop the merger. And during his years with the railroad, he was always a strong union man, unafraid to tell politicians and railroad officials exactly what was on his mind.

In both instances, his friends say, he was driven by the desire to make the railroads live up to their promise as public servants — companies that were given huge tracts of public land in exchange for a pledge to provide the best possible rail service to the areas they served. He thinks the Burlington Northern, now the Burlington Northern Santa Fe, failed that trust.

By contrast, he has nothing but praise for Missoula industrialist Dennis Washington, whose Montana Rail Link leases the line between Billings and Spokane from BNSF.

"That's the best thing that's happened in Livingston since the merger is Montana Rail Link — they serve the public," McGee says.

McGee was also a big force in establishing, in 1987, the Livingston Depot Center Museum, which now displays many of his photographs and pieces of train memorabilia.

But McGee says his "crowning achievement" was giving a narrated slide presentation of his photographs at the Northern Pacific Railway Historical Association in Fargo, N.D., earlier this year. Though the presentation was supposed to last an hour or an hour and a half, McGee had a story for every slide, and it stretched to more than three hours.

Tarbox, the president of the Northern Pacific Railway Historical Association, said McGee had to strain to see what slide was on the screen, but as soon as knew, the tales just flowed.

"They sat there for three hours and 30 minutes, and nobody left the room," McGee said. "That's what I call getting people's attention."

He got people's attention with some of his other historical work, including his researches into the Bozeman Trail in the Park County area. He said he first heard about the pioneer trail about 1970, while showing slides to another historical group, and he got so interested that he made himself something of a local expert.

"I had historians over at this university in Bozeman following me around like a dog," he said.

It was only recently that he figured out what he'd been doing all these years.

"I've been a historian, I guess, all my life, but I didn't know it."

Originally published October 2, 2005, in The Billings Gazette

THE BAR DIAMOND RANCH

NORTH OF BILLINGS — From atop a high ridge north-west of Billings, Vince Carpenter and Jack Dietrich are looking out over an immense, breathtaking landscape. Most of what they're looking at is within the boundaries of their Bar Diamond Ranch. Hundreds of calves are grazing on the pastures below, and beyond them hills studded with ponderosa pine roll off toward the horizon. Meadowlarks are trilling and juniper bushes are heavy with berries, heavier than Carpenter ever remembers seeing them. Near the edge of a high cliff, Carpenter and Dietrich have just been looking at a carefully constructed circle, about 15 feet across, made of stacks of sandstone slabs. Carpenter thinks it may be a place where American Indians used to gather for ceremonial purposes. He points to a faint track that leads down to the base of the hill, and from there to a few ancient tepee rings.

Dietrich has been to the ranch countless times over the past 40 years, but never to this spot before. After looking at the circle of stones, he wanders off by himself to another point on the ridge, standing in a steady breeze as he gazes into the distance.

After a few moments, Carpenter breaks the silence, shouting out, "Maybe we better not sell, Jack."

Dietrich turns around, looking surprised. "I was just thinking that, seriously," he says. "I was thinking, what in the hell are we doing selling?"

Serious or not, it is only a passing spell of remorse. The decision has been made. They will soon start advertising in regional publications, offering for sale a 16,000-acre ranch that is one of the larger private land holdings in Yellowstone County. The sale will break up a partnership that began at a holiday gathering more than 40 years ago, a partnership that knitted two families together and that over the years has done nothing to diminish the friendship of Jack and Vince.

The decision to sell was helped along by the steady expansion of the city, the increasing price of land and the likelihood that a highway — the proposed north bypass — will someday go through the ranch. But the decision was also prompted by the realization that Carpenter, who turns 86 in July, and Dietrich, who turns 82 in August, aren't going to be around forever.

They gradually came to the conclusion that it wouldn't be fair to ask any one member of the family to continue running the ranch with everyone in both extended families constantly looking over his shoulder. The person under such scrutiny undoubtedly would have been Vince's son, Larry Carpenter, who has lived on the ranch year-round since 1969.

Larry Carpenter said the two patriarchs, whatever fleeting regrets they may have expressed on their recent tour of the ranch, are fairly well reconciled to the sale. That's more than he can say for himself.

"I don't think it's really hit me yet," he said. "I'm the one that's going to really have a hard time because I've put my whole life into it."

Jack Dietrich's grandfather came out to Montana from New Hampshire in the late 1880s and had a sheep ranch in the Sweetgrass Hills near Helena. Jack grew up in Deer Lodge and moved to Billings in 1955 to join the Crowley law firm, which he was with long enough for it to become Crowley, Haughey, Hanson, Toole & Dietrich.

Vince Carpenter is a Minnesotan by birth, but his wife's grandfather was Col. H.W. Rowley, a successful entrepreneur in early-day Billings. Between visits to her family and to the cabin they bought near Red Lodge, the Carpenters came often to Billings. At the cabin, their next-door neighbors were the Dietrichs, and the two families quickly grew close.

Jack had some familiarity with ranching on the family spread, and Vince, who loved animals and whose family had always had a huge garden, thought he'd like to give ranching a try. They looked into buying a ranch south of Red Lodge but decided against it. Then Frank Mackey's place, the Bar Diamond Ranch north of Billings, came on the market. It was 1963, and the Carpenters were in Montana for the Christmas holidays. Vince and his wife, Janet, were planning to head back to Minnesota on New Year's Day, but they decided to have a look at the Mackey place first. Accompanied by Jack and his wife, Anne, they toured the southern end of the ranch. There was snow on the ground, and it was cold. But they saw sage hens and antelope, and they fell in love with the high, lonesome beauty of the land.

"We thought, this is the greatest place in the world," Jack said. "The good Lord had his arms around us."

That was all it took. By February 1964, they had closed on a 20,000-acre ranch. In the early years, the ranch was managed by Dale Wright, who had been Mackey's ranch foreman, with help from John Gelock, whose family had homesteaded in the area in 1909. Mackey, originally a sheep man, had come north from the St. Xavier area in the 1930s and had begun buying up abandoned homesteads north of Billings. Eventually, he put together a 90,000-acre ranch that stretched from the Rimrocks above Billings to the Bull Mountains south of Roundup. The Dietrichs and Carpenters had purchased the southern portion of the ranch.

Vince and his family continued to live in Minnesota, where Vince was a music teacher at Macalester College in St. Paul for 21 years, but the call of the ranch finally lured him away.

"It was a rude awakening," he said. "We came out in '68, and that was one of the worst winters they ever had out there." It was bitterly cold day after day, and the snow was thick. Vince remembers going out before dawn in long underwear, jeans, coveralls, a wool hat, double-lined gloves and insulated boots. They worked all day to keep the cattle fed and watered, and for lunch they'd stop in at a hand's place, where his wife made chicken-fried steaks and heaps of greasy fried potatoes.

"The only thing we took off was our gloves," he said. "We

even left our hats on, we were so cold. That was my introduction to ranching. I thought, boy, what have I done?"

Some folks who lived in the area asked the same question, figuring Vince couldn't stand the ranching life for long.

"People used to think we were nuts," Larry Carpenter said. "We heard secondhand that up at the M&M Bar at Acton, which was the original bar up there, that people used to refer to my dad as 'that fiddle player from Minnesota,' and what a fool he must be. But you know, by God, he showed 'em. He proved 'em wrong."

While Larry and his family continued to live on the ranch, for many years in an old bunkhouse and then in a newly built home, Vince and Janet always lived in Billings. For Vince, it was a 25-minute commute in the old days, when Main Street through what is now the Heights was virtually empty of cars. He worked out there every day and, with Larry, made most of the day-to-day decisions at the ranch. Jack Dietrich said he used to go out to the ranch on weekends and "play cowboy and help feed. I had the best of all worlds."

For their families — Jack has five children and Vince has three — the ranch was always a place where they could get away from the city for a quick visit or a longer stay. They used to swim in the reservoirs in the summer and skate on them in the winter. It was also the place for family gatherings and barbecues, for hiking and riding horses, trap shooting and cutting Christmas trees. And they all helped out with ranch chores over the years.

Dr. Janet Dietrich, one of Jack's three daughters, who is a gynecologist in Billings, said it was a luxury to have a ranch that always felt like her backyard. She said she has never pretended to be a real rancher, but having fed cattle, stacked hay and rounded up cows on horseback, she had a sense of what it was to be one.

"At least I've had the privilege to have a glimpse of those things," she said.

Janet said that before she married Dan Erikson, she told him: "If we're going to get married and this is going to be a long-term relationship, you have to know this land. This is important." He must have believed her. He ended up working on the ranch, living with Larry, for a year before they wed.

Having the ranch so near gave her and other members of the

two families a chance to experience things that would have been foreign to most people growing up in Billings, Janet Dietrich said. She takes it for granted that she is familiar with a coyote's call, a meadowlark's singsong chirping and the mating dance of sharp-tailed grouse and sage grouse. And as Billings continued to expand and change, the ranch remained essentially the same.

"It's changed precious little in the 40-plus years we've owned it," Janet said. If Mackey were to come back and see it now, she said, "I don't think he would be aware of significant changes."

Most years, the Dietrichs and Carpenters ran about 500 head of cattle on the ranch and also grew some wheat. The sprawling ranch contains 41 pastures, eight water systems, multiple pumps and miles of underground piping.

In the late 1980s, Vince and Larry formed the Carpenter Livestock Co. They leased the land from the family-held corporation that owned the ranch and acquired all the livestock and machinery. Both families retained full access to the ranch, but Vince and Larry called the shots on its operation.

Since the ranch had been formed as a corporation, Jack and Vince used to constitute its board of directors. As their children got older, the board expanded and in recent years has included two of Jack's children, Janet and David, and two of Vince's, Larry and Mark. It was ultimately a decision of the whole board to sell the ranch. Although the Bar Diamond Ranch encompassed nearly 20,000 acres when the partners bought it 42 years ago, one chunk of it was sold off, and it now consists of 15,826 acres. That's still a lot of land — almost 25 square miles, two-thirds the size of the entire city of Billings. At its widest point it stretches from Highway 3 just below Acton most of the way to Highway 87 a little north of the Heights.

Jack said there had never been any pressure to sell the whole ranch before because it was known that the partners weren't interested in selling. There was, however, much interest from people wanting to buy some smaller chunks of land, those nearest the highway or the city of Billings, for development.

"There was a lot of pressure to carve off 160 acres, whatever," Jack said. "But we adopted a policy that we wouldn't sell it piecemeal. It was going to be sold as a unit."

That is still their hope. They know that sometime in the future, particularly if the north bypass is built through the ranch, the temptation to subdivide and develop the land will be irresistible. But for now, they're hoping to find a buyer who is willing to continue ranching for some years.

Larry is thinking of shaving 640 acres off the ranch — a section west of Highway 3 near Acton — where he can build a big shop and where he and his wife, Kris, can run their horses and keep their "pet cow." There is also the possibility that he could stay on for some time as ranch manager for whoever ends up buying the place. Then again, he said, only half joking, maybe nobody will want to buy it.

"If the ranch didn't sell, hey, I could deal with that."

Originally published May 28, 2006, in The Billings Gazette

WALKER JOHN, R.I.P.

BILLINGS — For most of his life, John Stambulich was a pretty regular guy. He loved to camp. He was an avid reader, and his favorite author was Stephen King. "It," based on a King novel, was one of his favorite movies.

He liked John Wayne movies, too, and his favorite television show was "Star Trek: The Next Generation." He even had a favorite episode, "Inner Light," which his wife got him for Christmas a few years ago.

He was a pool shooter, a bowler and a storyteller with a good memory for faces. He was born in Chicago in 1960 and moved to Billings with his family as a pre-schooler. He went to North Park School, to schools in Lockwood and then to Billings Senior High. He drove cow trucks and worked for various businesses as a cashier.

When he met Lori, his future wife, in Seattle, she was working at a self-service gas station where he was hired to work at a lube shop the owner had added on. They had two children together and lived in Lockwood, and Lori said John was "the most loving and wonderful person in the world."

And yet when John died of heart failure on Oct. 12, 2006, he dropped dead on the streets of downtown Billings where he had been living for the past year and a half.

John was known as "Walker John" among other homeless people and among the downtown workers who got to know him. He always shuffled along with his metal walker, which was slung with plastic grocery bags that carried his meager possessions. He had glasses and a beard, and he usually wore a hat.

He spent much of the day at the library or the Hub, a drop-in center run by the Mental Health Center. He slept where he could. That became more difficult after he gave up on the Montana Rescue Mission, where somebody stole his false teeth. He told me last winter, when I interviewed him for a story on homelessness in Billings, "I just curl up where it's warm."

Lisa Harmon knew John well. She is the director of the Downtown Billings Business Improvement District, and she is also the chairwoman of the Mayor's Committee on Homelessness. She called 911 for John a few times, most recently in September. She said John's death ought to make people stop and think.

"Here's a guy from our area who died stuck to the pavement," she said. "That's just unacceptable."

Harmon wasn't suggesting that we ignore the plight of people who came here from somewhere else. But she hopes that if people know some of the homeless are like John — local people who led normal lives until something went terribly wrong — we might be more inclined to help them.

So, what went wrong?

Lori, John's wife, said John didn't become homeless overnight. He suffered from diabetes and other health problems. Three years ago he slipped on a bathroom carpet and fractured his leg. A year later he fell on some ice and broke his hip. He had never been much of a drinker, but his injuries pushed him slowly into the habit, to the point where Lori said he simply couldn't live with his family, not with two children.

She did what she could to help him. She saw him two or three times a week, bought his cigarettes and toiletries and accompanied him anytime he went to see a doctor.

"It's not like I didn't love him," Lori said. "He and I were together almost 17 years."

But he couldn't straighten out and find a place to live, or a job, or any stability. And life on the street was hard. He fell, he got mugged, he got robbed. Fire Department records show that he was the subject of 12 emergency calls in the past four years, some of them predating his time on the streets. Emergency calls are the ones that involve a fire truck and an ambulance, at a minimum. The number doesn't include any times when he may have been treated as part of a call made on somebody else's behalf, and they don't begin to suggest what his emergency hospital treatment might have cost.

Lori said she and John's friends tried to help him, but their options were limited.

"He made the decision as to what he was going to do," she said. But she wishes something could be done to help people like John make the right decisions. That is more or less the kind of partial solution to chronic homelessness the mayor's committee is looking at. The idea, and it has been used elsewhere, is to give homeless people a place to live and the support they need to regain normal lives. It costs money up front and it looks like welfare gone wild to critics, but when the alternative is spending thousands or hundreds of thousands of dollars on emergency room care and endless police and fire time, maybe it won't look so bad.

Maybe. And maybe it won't work. But people like Harmon think we can do more than we're doing now. She became aware of that with a pang after John died. When she saw him this summer, she told him he needed to get his broken glasses fixed. The next time she saw him they were — put back together with layer upon layer of duct tape.

"I wished I had asked more of myself," she said, because she realized she knew dozens of people who gladly would have bought John a new pair of glasses. "I don't think we don't want to help. I think we don't know how."

Lori had John's remains cremated, as he had requested. And she planned to scatter his ashes on the Beartooth Pass, also at his request. It was something he talked about almost as soon as they met. He even used to joke that he'd probably die in the winter and she'd have to wait until the pass opened again.

"We will do that this spring," Lori said.

Originally published November 5, 2006, in The Billings Gazette

JULES KIMMETT:
FINDING A FATHER

FISHTAIL — Katy Martin's father was not an easy person
to love, to put it mildly.

Jules Kimmett was a violent, volatile taskmaster, given to
beating up on his wife and severely disciplining Katy and her
brother. After her parents divorced, Katy hardly saw her father
for years, and rarely more than once a year for a long time after
that. Her brother still can't forgive his father for the way he was
treated, and he refuses to have anything to do with him.

Not so with Katy. Beginning about the time she married Bill
Martin in 1980, her thoughts about her father, and about her
mother, an alcoholic in some ways even more troublesome than
her father, began to change. Katy realized that love must be un-
conditional, and that her parents had been shaped, as she had
been, by events beyond their control.

"I finally got old enough where I realized that's just the way
their lives were," she said. "Nobody's life is perfect. My dad did
the best he could, and so did my mom."

That realization helped her grow closer to both parents. It also motivated Katy to take her aged father under her wing when
he was no longer able to care for himself, bringing him from Cali-

fornia to live near her in Fishtail in 1997. That decision, in turn, led Katy to her father's collection of papers, photographs and memorabilia, and she began to explore the life of a man she hardly knew. She said she never had a chance to ask her father about the past when she lived with him.

"Life was pretty crazy," she said. "All I worried about was surviving."

By the time she became interested in her parents' past, her mother wouldn't talk and her father, debilitated by Alzheimer's disease, couldn't. Though there are still many gaps in her knowledge of her father's life — she's not even sure when he was born — she learned more about his career as a professional baseball player, his service in World War II and his years as a political gadfly who once made a run for governor of California. Those discoveries, matched with the joy she gets from a relationship that could have been allowed to fade away, reaffirmed her decision to bring her father back into her life.

"He's my dad," she says. "He got older and somebody had to take care of him, so that was my responsibility."

From what Katy has been able to piece together, her father's parents were Russian Jews who came to the United States when Jules was 6 months old. His mother died soon after the family settled in Boston and his father and stepmother had four more children. Katy thinks her father's real name was Harry Green, shortened from Greenvitch.

Jules apparently felt like the black sheep of the family, and he chafed at his father's plans to have him follow in his footsteps and become a tailor. Instead, at 17, he went off on his own and became a professional baseball player. Because he was a minor and his father wouldn't give his permission, he lied about his age and adopted a new name. "Jules" came from Jules Verne, the author of his favorite book, "20,000 Leagues Under the Sea," and "Kimmett" from the last name of a good friend.

He later lied about his age — this time making himself younger — so he could enlist during World War II. Those two large falsehoods, combined with some smaller ones, make it hard to know just how old Jules is. Katy said Social Security had two birth dates for her father, and the Army Air Corps had another. But her father also used to say he was 5 years older than her mother, whose age Katy knew. Based on that, Katy thinks her father is 97. You could hardly guess his age to look at him now. His face is weathered and his few remaining teeth jut out at odd angles, but his wide smile and the impishness around his eyes make him look younger, as does his wiry physique. That compact frame, and a touch of that impishness, is evident in an undated photograph showing Jules in a Rebels baseball uniform. Katy doesn't know where the Rebels played or when the photo was taken. She doesn't even remember where she got it.

Documents Katy found in her father's collection revealed that he was playing for Charleston, S.C., in 1946, and in 1947 the "Baseball Guide and Record Book" lists him as a utility player in the South Atlantic League. It also says that in 1945 he played for a team in Lincoln, Neb., and was an All-American selection that year. He told people he was a left-handed pitcher, but the baseball guide lists him as a utility player. He apparently never played in the big leagues. In his wallet he still carries a brass plate, worn and corroded and slightly bent, from the Association of Professional Baseball Players of America. Undated, it confers upon him a life membership in the association.

Jules always used to say that he enlisted in the Army Air Corps on Dec. 8, 1941, the day after Japan attacked Pearl Harbor, and that he served as a tailgunner on a bomber. But his "separation qualification record," which was included with his discharge papers, says he enlisted on Jan. 16, 1942, and served as a radio mechanic. There is no mention of being a tailgunner.

"He could have lied about that, too," Katy said with a shrug.

Katy doesn't know much about Jules' personal life before he met her mother, but when she moved him out of his apartment in California she found 15 old-fashioned tailor-made suits with wide lapels in his closet. The fact that he hung onto them for so long, and spent so much on them when he was younger, told Katy that her father was something of a dandy, and probably something of a ladies' man. Jules met his future wife, Alice, in 1946. Katy's brother, Larry, was born to the couple a year later, and Katy in 1949. Katy said her mother was born in South Carolina and had a hard life. At 16, she was married off to a 30-year-old man, with whom she had three children. Her mother never told Jules about the earlier marriage or the children, but Jules found out somehow.

Katy said her first memory is of watching her father confront her mother with knowledge of her past. Katy said he put his fist through a wall and screamed at her mother, "This is what will happen to you if you lie to me again."

Her parents fought all the time, and her mother was usually drunk.

"I suppose it was a double-edged sword," Katy said. "He drove her to drink and she drove him crazy."

When she and Larry were very young and her parents were going through one of their periodic separations, Jules came to their house during the day — Katy doesn't remember where they were living then with her mother — and took them to Atlanta to live with him. Her mother didn't come looking for them right away. First she saved up enough money to buy a gun. When she had one she went to Atlanta, found Jules' place, then waited through the afternoon for Jules to get off work. When Jules entered his apartment, she was standing there with the handgun, which she brandished as she threatened to kill him if he ever took the kids again. Obviously, their mother wasn't easy to live with, either, but Katy and her brother didn't miss their father much.

"My dad was pretty cruel when he was younger," she said. Once, when Larry hit Katy in the head with a rock, Jules beat him so savagely with a belt that Katy swears it nearly killed her brother.

Her parents finally divorced in 1959, when Katy was 10. After briefly running away from home at 16, Katy, then living in North Hollywood, Calif., moved in with a friend's family for eight months. After that, she lived with her high school vice principal, whose daughters Katy knew. Katy stayed there until graduating from high school, and in 1969 she got married. Her father, whom she'd seen every six months or so after high school, gave her away. She continued seeing him two or three times a year while she was living in California. Over the years, she also sent him a card on Father's Day.

"I remember every year trying to find a card that said something truthful," she said, meaning she never sent a card to "a loving father," or "the best father in the world."

Katy realizes now that one thing she learned from her harsh

childhood was how to survive, and somehow all her troubles made her want to help other people. That might explain why she worked as a special education teacher, and why she and some of her friends started a rape hot line and counseling center in the mid-1970s. She had been divorced for five years when she met Bill. She was working on battered women's issues and was speaking to a service club to which Bill belonged. After they got married in 1980, Katy continued to visit her father regularly. The visits dropped off to once a year when she and Bill moved to Lake Tahoe in 1987 and then retired to Fishtail six years later.

In 1997, she tried to reach her father but found out that his phone had been disconnected. She learned that he hadn't paid his phone bill, which was unlike him, and his landlord told Katy that he needed to be reminded to pay his rent. "It started to become clear that things were really going downhill," she said. Burbank by then had become Jules' life, but Katy said he didn't squawk about moving to Montana. As independent as he was, and as ornery, she figures he knew he needed help.

Among the materials recovered from his apartment was a videotape of a documentary on Jules, made in 1978 for Community Television of Southern California. It was another eye-opener. Jules had worked for years as a janitor at Valley College in Van Nuys, Calif., but his avocation was attending, as often as he could, meetings of the Los Angeles School Board, the L.A. City Council, the County Board of Supervisors, the Burbank City Council and the Community College Board of Trustees. With his heavy Boston accent and his folksy style, not to mention his homespun wisdom and his willingness to expound at length on any and all subjects, he apparently became a well-known local character, part sage and part annoying crank. In videotaped appearances before the government boards, and in interviews with the makers of the documentary, he took great pride in tossing out quotations from Shakespeare, Twain, Locke, Milton and other famous authors.

At one point, addressing the filmmaker, Jules reels off a list of great writers and then says, "It's good reading. Those bastards are solid." According to the documentary, Jules was also one of many people to challenge Gov. Edmund "Pat" Brown during Brown's re-election campaign in 1962. Brown won, but Jules polled a respectable 82,000 votes.

When Jules came to live in Fishtail, where Bill and Katy now own the Fishtail General Store, he lived down the street from his daughter. A year later, Bill's parents also moved to town, settling in across the street. Though Jules was almost 90 when he came to Montana, he was still fit and energetic, accustomed to taking daily walks of up to 15 miles. That wasn't so bad at first, but as his Alzheimer's got worse, he'd occasionally set out too late in the day, sometimes as late as 5 p.m. Katy and Bill might get a call from a friend saying her father was 10 miles from home and it was getting dark.

"Then he started hitchhiking," Katy said. He'd get picked up and would always ask to be taken "to the bank." So people would drop him off at the bank in Absarokee, where the employees would dutifully call the Martins, or drive Jules home themselves. It finally became obvious four years ago that he could no longer take care of himself. Katy and Bill looked at care facilities all over Billings but settled on the Beartooth Manor in Columbus because it was close and the people seemed nice.

Katy's mother, who ended up marrying four or five more times after leaving Jules, died two years ago, and Bill's parents both died last year. Katy feels more attached to her father all the time and visits him in Columbus as often as she can. Katy said she was thinking mainly about her father when she decided to take care of him in his old age, but she has benefited as much as he has.

"So maybe that forgiveness was something God meant me to do," she said. "After that, my life was just totally different."

Originally published June 20, 2004, in The Billings Gazette

JEFF HANSEN:
THE SOUNDS OF SOLACE

BILLINGS — In the gathering darkness of a Friday afternoon in January, Jeff Hansen is serenading Marilyn Neill in her
hospital room at St. Vincent Healthcare in Billings.

On his mountain dulcimer, a four-stringed instrument that
produces a sweet, airy sound reminiscent of a harp or a maybe a
harpsichord, Jeff is playing "From All That Dwell Below the
Skies," one of the hundreds of Lutheran hymns he first heard in
church as a boy.

Marilyn, a leukemia patient, is sitting in an easy chair her
husband brought up from their home in Buffalo, Wyo. This is her
33rd day at St. Vincent, and the chair, a touch of home comfort,
makes her hospital stay easier to bear.

So does the dulcimer music, which Jeff plays with an intense,
serious look on his face, focusing on his left hand as it dances
through chord changes and runs up and down the neck of the
instrument cradled in his lap. The air of seriousness melts away at
the end of the song, when Jeff shakes the cramps out of his left
hand, leans back and allows a smile to spread across his face.

A hospital worker walks into the room just then and asks
Marilyn how she's doing.

Marilyn slowly opens her eyes and says, "I'm just so relaxed. I feel like I went to heaven and back."

That seems appropriate. Jeff says the hymn that inspires him to play at St. Vincent is Johann Olearius' "Comfort, Comfort Ye My People," a verse of which reads, "Comfort those who sit in darkness, Mourning 'neath their sorrows' load."

Jeff bears a similar burden, creating an almost palpable bond with his listeners. He had testicular cancer — actually a rare combination of two types of cancer — that was caught early in October 2001.

"That thing, I think, is gone," he says. "All the lymph nodes are gone. They tore me up pretty good getting them all out."

A larger problem is the brain tumor he has lived with since he was 17, and which is considered inoperable because it is too close to the hypothalamus. Jeff, 29, said doctors have been trying to find the right drug or drugs to treat the tumor, but, in the meantime, he is unable to drive, unable to work, unable to do much of anything but play music.

He lives with his parents and sleeps a lot, sometimes for 24 hours straight. He has been told he'll be able to work again when he goes six months without blacking out, but he has dizzy spells every day and blacks out at least once a week.

"Every once in a while I'll hit the ground, and when I wake up I won't know where I was," he says.

Jeff started playing the dulcimer when he was 10, after his father was given a crudely made instrument as a gift. But he didn't get serious about the dulcimer until six years ago, when he bought an Arkansas-made McSpadden mountain dulcimer and began to expand his repertoire.

That same year, Jeff's grandmother died. "Just to cope, I got my great-aunt's hymnal out. Upstairs, before I went to bed, I said, 'I'm going to learn these old hymns I remember.' "

He had taken piano lessons through the third grade and retained enough knowledge to figure out at least the melody of the hymns, which he translates into notes and chords on the dulcimer. He doesn't sing when he plays, letting the dulcimer speak for itself.

He figures he knows more than 200 hymns now, 70 of them by heart, most of them old German songs but also a fair number from England, Scotland and other countries. He loves the music, and he loves talking about the hymns.

Sitting with Marilyn in her third-floor hospital room, pausing between songs, Jeff relates a story about Martin Luther and then speaks of John Huss, the Czech religious reformer burned at the stake for heresy in 1415. "Nearer My God to Thee" reminds Jeff of how, in the movie "Titanic," the orchestra played that song as the great ship went down.

"Instead of chaos," Jeff says, recalling the scene, "there's tranquility."

Jeff's stint as an informal music therapist began in the fall of 2002. He had gotten in the habit of bringing his dulcimer with him when he attended a cancer support group that met Friday mornings across the street from St. Vincent's main building, because sometimes he'd have to wait an hour or two afterward for his mother to give him a ride home.

He would have lunch in the Subway on the second floor of the medical building, then play his dulcimer in a wide corridor next to the restaurant, where the high, skylighted ceilings made for good acoustics.

One day, other members of his support group prevailed on him to close a session with a hymn. That quickly became a tradition, and before long two of the group facilitators suggested that he share his talents with a wider audience.

It is now a Friday ritual for Jeff: support group from 10:30 to noon, a little warming up in the corridor, lunch at Subway and then anywhere from five to eight hours playing for other patients, usually on the third-floor oncology ward.

Jeff stands an imposing 6-feet-8, but he speaks quietly. Hunched over his dulcimer, he radiates a peacefulness that is as soothing as the music. Even in below-zero weather he usually wears a short-sleeve knit shirt and shorts. The tumor near his hypothalamus threw off his internal thermostat and usually makes him overheated.

Some Friday nights he'll go straight from the hospital to jam sessions sponsored by the Yellowstone Bluegrass Association in the Lincoln Center. All that playing usually wipes him out. It might take him two or three days to recover his strength. Spiritually, though, it's rejuvenating.

"If I hadn't had exposure to the hymns, I think I'd probably be a lost cause," he says.

He has noticed something similar among the people for whom he plays. "The ones that are at peace have that spirituality," he says.

Marilyn tells Jeff that her leukemia has only strengthened her faith.

"I learned a lot about trust, about trust in God," she says. "I feel like I've been put to the test."

Jeff nods and tells her, "If I hadn't gotten sick, I'd probably be sitting on the top floor of the First Interstate in a cubicle." He laughs and then continues. "I was really into money when I was a teenager; I thought that was cool. Then I got sick, and my priorities kind of changed."

He elaborates later, telling how, during high school in Iowa, he got involved in a stock-market game and discovered a knack for picking winners. He kept playing the market after moving to Billings with his family when he was a junior, and he assumed that he'd eventually become a broker, a mutual-fund manager or something along those lines.

Now he lives day to day, saving his strength for Fridays, hoping for an improvement in his condition.

"I keep a positive outlook," he says. "I'm not really afraid of anything."

For Marilyn, he plays another hymn, "O for a Thousand Tongues to Sing." When he is done, the melody still lingering in the air, he looks toward the ceiling with a dreamy look in his eyes.

He says, "I kind of wonder what those old composers would think if they were here, knowing they were helping people."

Originally published February 8, 2004, in The Billings Gazette

ACKNOWLEDGMENTS

I thank the publications that allowed me to pursue these stories and gave me the permission to reprint them here. My thanks in particular to The Billings Gazette, where I have worked for the past 22 years, most of them as a reporter and columnist. My editors have given me a degree of freedom increasingly rare in a business increasingly constrained, and I hope they know how much it has meant to me.

One of the luckiest breaks in my years in the newspaper business is that I've always had good editors, none better than my friend Tom Tollefson, who has been editing my stories for the past 15 years. There is hardly a piece in this book that has not been improved by his pencil, his perspective, his patience.

They say a writer's first obligation is to satisfy himself. But I am often quite lazy and easily satisfied, so it is better for me to aim at satisfying Tom, or at least trying not to disappoint him.

ABOUT THE AUTHOR

Ed Kemmick is a Minnesota native who has lived in Montana for most of the past 38 years. He has worked for newspapers in Butte, Mont., and St. Paul, Minn., and has been with The Billings Gazette since 1989. At The Gazette, he was an editor for seven years before going back to reporting in 1996. He has also written a Sunday column, *City Lights*, since 2000. He and his wife, Lisa, have three daughters.

CPSIA information can be obtained at www.ICGtesting.com
Printed in the USA
LVOW121629301011

252730LV00003B/5/P